designer**guys**

designer**guys**
Finding your personal style

Chris Hyndman and Steven Sabados

A Smith Sherman Book
produced in conjunction with WestWind Pictures Ltd.
and published by McClelland & Stewart Ltd.

M&S

Cloth edition published 2002.
Trade paperback edition 2004.

Created by WestWind Pictures Ltd. and Smith Sherman Books Inc.
designer**guys** is a trademark of Mary Darling

National Library of Canada Cataloguing in Publication

Hyndman, Chris
   Designerguys : finding your personal style / Chris Hyndman and Steven Sabados.

Includes index.
ISBN 0-7710-4288-4 (bound).–ISBN 0-7710-4201-9 (pbk.)

1. Interior decoration. 2. Dwellings--Remodeling. I. Sabados, Steven II. Title.
HQ2042.H95 2002   747   C2002-903788-3

McClelland & Stewart Ltd.
The Canadian Publishers
481 University Avenue
Toronto, Ontario
M5G 2E9
www.mcclelland.com

PHOTOGRAPHY BY SHANNON HILL

FRONT JACKET PHOTO AND PHOTO PAGE 207 BY TIM LEYES, FANDANGO FILMS

EDITORIAL DEVELOPMENT BY CAROL SHERMAN

DESIGN AND PAGE COMPOSITION BY PAGEWAVE GRAPHICS INC.

COLOUR SEPARATIONS BY COLOUR TECHNOLOGIES, TORONTO

1 2 3 4 5 TWP 08 07 06 05 04

PRINTED AND BOUND IN SINGAPORE

We dedicate this book to our parents for giving us the confidence to follow our dreams.

Thanks to WestWind Pictures and the entire production team of designer**guys** who helped make those dreams come true.

Contents

7

Our Personal Styles Then and Now

STYLE TO ME is comfort. I don't just mean "those jeans are too tight and I can't bend over" kind of comfort, I'm talking comfortable in your own skin. I think style is based on being proud, confident and comfortable with who you are.

I remember when I was fourteen years old, my mom came down the stairs dressed for a party in a canary yellow dress and matching three-toned pumps. Everyone thought she looked beautiful in that outfit, especially me. She was a vision. I noticed her body language, though, was different — she didn't seem to be her confident self. I asked her what was wrong? She replied, "I don't feel comfortable in this dress. People are going to stare at me." I thought that was the whole point. Don't you want people to stare at you? I know I do, although I guess I would have gotten a lot more looks than even I could have handled if I had worn that yellow dress to an event. But for my mother, who usually was confident, that wasn't the point. She wanted to feel comfortable and she didn't. What makes one person comfortable doesn't necessarily make another person feel that way. Being true to who you are makes you comfortable, and that's all part of personal style.

When you are comfortable in all aspects of your life, then you have mastered your own personal style. I have made my life comfortable in several ways. When I get up in the morning, I like to be able to find everything easily or I become frustrated. My clothes are color coordinated and easy to match. My home has a monochromatic scheme, so I don't get over-stimulated. My kitchen looks good, but I don't cook. Are you getting the point? All these things have become my personal style. With all of them in place, I am comfortable.

When you are trying to be somebody else, which I have done in the past, you will lack personal style. When you are comfortable with who you are and what you are projecting, then your body language screams COOL. I don't mean cool as in icy, I mean cool as in confident.

The most important thing to me is to be true to who you are. I remember when I moved to the big city. All I wanted was to be everything that I saw and forget everything that I was. There were more clothes, parties, fabulous people, smart cars and luxurious homes than I ever could have imagined. To start on my journey to be cool was overwhelming, exciting and, most of all, terrifying. I quickly forgot about my mother's comfortable home, my calm way of life and any sense of security. Because of designer**guys**, I have met people from all walks of life including homeowners, editors of fashion magazines, real estate agents, actresses, stay-at-home moms, television producers and presidents of companies. I have a beautiful home, lots of clothes and more shoes than any man should be allowed. I guess that I have become everything I wanted to be. But wouldn't you know it. My life in Newfoundland and that small-town boy that I was is still there more than ever. Everything that I left behind is becoming more important to me now. Laughter, kindness, humility and humanity are commonplace when you grow up in a small town. I now realize that forgetting the past to try to create a future does not necessarily work. My twenty years in a small town combined with my fifteen years in a big town have all played a part in creating my personal style and who I am today. Maybe that is why I am craving a small house in the country, with family and friends around me to supply me with all the comfort and security I could ever imagine.

CHRIS HYNDMAN

STYLE COMES IN many forms — subtle to the most outrageous — and a person's style definitely changes with the years. I still look back at my high school pictures in utter embarrassment. What was I thinking with those velour shirts and bell bottom "painter pants"? But how stylish I thought I was. Now I find myself to be a sponge, constantly taking in visual information. With all this information I have developed a personal style that expresses who I am. I like to wear flashy clothing, but not too flashy that I will stand out too much. I like to decorate in a way that is creative but not over the top. All these things are an expression of my personality. I do not like to stand out in a crowd, but I do have a pair of yellow boots, which I think are fun and show my sense of humor. (Remember the orange belt I've worn on several of our shows?) Ultimately, I do not take myself too seriously and I think that comes through with my personal style. I enjoy having fun and like to project that image, even though I sometimes appear too stuffy and serious — after all, I don't think it's so bad to have a split personality, do you?

The most important thing I can say about my experiences is to listen to yourself and never be discouraged. Sure, you can still listen to your neighbor's advice, but ultimately the choices are yours. If we all didn't have unique personal styles, then everyone's houses would look the same — and I would be out of a job!

When I was a child growing up in a modest home in a small town in Ontario, my mother was a creative genius at keeping us four kids, not only busy, but looking good. She would sew us elaborate outfits (although I was forced to wear my sisters' hand-me-downs). She would gather us around the kitchen table on a rainy day for craft sessions. I always looked forward to those rainy days when Mom would pull out the box of crayons, glue sticks, old wallpaper books and allow our little minds to creatively run wild. I knew then that if I could do this every day, I would be a happy boy. I would sit for hours in my bedroom gluing together egg cartons and paper-towel rolls creating rocket ships or a futuristic hot rod car.

Even at birthdays I remember standing on a stool in the kitchen beside my mom, helping her decorate four-tier cakes with multicolored icing and carefully crafting the perfect icing-sugar rose. My mother taught me well. How was I to know that all this knowledge my mom was giving me was actually developing my own creative style? A lot of who you are comes from your past and should never be ignored. You actually have style at an early age. I even remember once baking bread with my mom. While she took me through the stages of bread making, I said, "Can we put food coloring in the dough?" She asked, "Why?" And I replied, "I would like to have blue toast." She gladly passed me the bottle of food coloring and watched my creative juices flow. I have to thank my mom for allowing me to be creative on all levels — after all, why can't toast be blue?

Although I haven't made blue bread since (but once in art college I dyed my hair blue), I was always encouraged to color outside the lines. Personal style is a lot like that. Each of us is striving for individuality. The differences in all of us are what make the world such a colorful place.

STEVEN SABADOS

Finding Your Personal Style

WE BELIEVE THAT everyone has a personal style. It's an expression of who you are. By defining your own personal style you'll be able to pull your look together, whether it is buying clothes, entertaining or home décor. We're here to give you the confidence to find your personal style and then, once you have defined it, how to express it.

Confidence and intimidation are probably the two most important concepts to address when it comes to defining your personal style. In a nutshell, if you are confident about who you are, then you won't be intimidated. It's that simple. How to be confident? That's the million-dollar question. We can guide you with some decorating know-how, some dos and don'ts and examples of other people's dilemmas, but in the end it really comes down to something as obvious as knowing yourself. Throughout the book you'll find lots of people who are just like you, going through the process of defining his or her personal style.

When we talk about personal style we're not talking about just one thing. We're talking about everything from what's in your closet to how you live. Look at every aspect of your lifestyle, and we mean everything, from what cars you are attracted to, restaurants you like to go to, type of foods you like to eat, to the colors and clothing and textures you wear. Personal style is huge to us — it's what makes you an individual. So, before you do anything else, look at your lifestyle and be true to it.

designer**guy** secret / STEVEN

I used to live in an all-white space because that's what I thought I wanted. Everything in the space was white – white sofas, white everything, the whole room was white. But I have a huge black Great Dane and I like to entertain. It made life very difficult to have white everything. The dog got on the sofa; red wine spilled one too many times. I got sick of it. I got frustrated trying to project an image to people that I lived in this pristine white home that required constant maintenance. It drove me bananas. So how you live, your lifestyle, is your personal style, too.

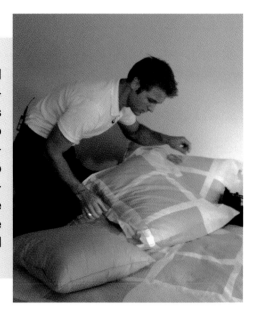

Many people go to decorators because they lack the confidence to decorate their space themselves and they need a lot of hand-holding. They have fears about "keeping up with the Joneses" and trying to be current, never looking passé. Obviously, outside of your wardrobe, your interior is one of the biggest reflections of who you are.

You are constantly being visually bombarded and these images, both in fashion and decorating, are always changing, which can be very intimidating. You think you've established a look and then all of a sudden it flips and you think you're out of style. Well, that's not necessarily the case. If you like it and it's your personal style, be happy with it. You can still bring things into your space or your wardrobe that are current. It's really about figuring out exactly how you live in that space and not worrying about what's hot and what isn't. There really is no such thing as what's hot anyway, because what's hot is your lifestyle, whatever it is.

We're not always in the position of knowing what we like and don't like. It takes time to get there. We're always moving toward it and are often surprised by how things change from year to year. We look at something we wore one year or placed on our windows the next and can't believe it. But that's growing and that's good.

designer**guy** secret / CHRIS

I used to decorate to keep up with my friends, who always had more beautiful homes and clothes and more expensive cars than I did. I was constantly comparing myself to them and never inviting them over to my house because I didn't think it was good enough. Obviously, I wasn't comfortable with my space because I was trying to decorate it for everybody else. Finally I just woke up one day and looked at my living room that I had just decorated and I loved what I had done. I thought it was beautiful. It gave me pleasure. I finally realized what was important: I had to be happy in my own space first.

Look in Your Closet

Looking in your closet is a great first step in defining your personal style because what you find there helps reflect who you are. We've decorated hundreds of homes and looked in as many closets and we've learned a few things about what's in there. This isn't rocket science and we're not saying we're always right, but in our experience, your clothes can tell you a lot about your decorating style.

When you look in your closet, you might see a variety of different colors there, but personal style is not a color scheme. When you look in your closet, you are looking for certain styles — the cut of your clothes, the fabrics, the designs. Do you have a lot of pattern? Are your skirts short? Are your pants wide? Are your suits pinstriped? Are they current? Are your clothes classics?

Your closet may reflect more about texture than color and pattern. If you don't have a lot of florals or stripes, but you do have different textures such as wools, satins and linens, it may translate into your surroundings.

Skirting the Issue

Looking at skirt styles in your closet is one great way to define your personal style. Of course, being two guys, we don't have any skirts in our closets, but we do have some opinions about what they might mean when they hang in yours.

The short skirt says that you are a little bit daring, especially if it's all short skirts in your closet. You are exciting and slightly on the wild side. This probably translates into a flashy, unusual room with something that catches your eye immediately such as brightly colored artwork or furniture. You're not afraid to be bold in your decorating — perhaps a bright red chair in the corner and a glass table with chrome legs on top of a leopard-skin rug. It might be mixed with something that is either undersized or oversized — say a huge red velvet joker-style chair, which you can't help but notice. And wearing a short skirt does the same thing. You're showing your legs. You're confident no matter what, or you just have great legs.

If most of your skirts are just below the knee and they're always that length and they never change, then you're probably a little more conservative and interested in textures rather than colors. You'd be someone who chooses safer styles in furniture such as a square arm on a sofa or something a little more traditional. You're not interested in introducing a bright color scheme into a room and possibly lean to a monochromatic look. You might have a little more wood in

your space — such as a wooden coffee table rather than a high-tech glass one. Maybe a little more French Country. Your skirts are probably in wools and linens, as are the fabrics in your home.

If you're someone who has every length in your closet — long, short, medium — then you are most likely a trend follower. You know what's happening. If one year a pillow comes out with beads all over it or bright fuchsia is the hot color, you'll have it on top of your Ultrasuede® couch. You bought the micro-mini the year it was in and then the below-the-knee skirt the next year when it came out. Although you keep them all and wear them all, you most likely wear the current ones the most.

A Man's World

We're not just talking about women's closets here, either. A man's fashion sense can help him define his decorating style as well. So, men, when you look in your closets, do you see lots of vibrant bold ties? Are they in the latest width? Do you have trendy shoes? If you have the latest width tie, shirts with French cuffs that are hot for the season or maybe a pair of red bowling shoes, then you're a contemporary fellow, possibly willing to change your space often because you're into the latest look.

If your closet contains classic suits, alligator belts and conservative ties, then your decorating style might be more traditional. If there's lots of color and pattern in your closet, maybe you're a little bit more eclectic — you enjoy a Hawaiian shirt on weekends and maybe a casual business suit during the day. And look to see if there's a sense of humor there — a taste for bright orange belts and yellow running shoes might be reflected in your home.

Don't see a lot of color there, but many different textures and tone-on-tone pattern? Perhaps you prefer more of a monochromatic look and love the look and feel of luxurious fabrics. The latest styles for home furnishings borrow from fabrics found in men's wardrobes — cashmere, tweed and linen — all can be transferred into throws, sofas and window treatments throughout your home.

designer**guy** secret / STEVEN

When I look in my closet there's tons of color there. I love pumpkin orange shirts and bright yellow boots. I like to be a little more flamboyant and flashy in my dress and try to reflect this in my environment. Even though I enjoy a monochromatic space, I really enjoy things with color and whimsy and a sense of surprise. In my home I like to accessorize with hits of color. For instance, a bright red pillow sits on top of my black-buttoned leather sofa and I've had my eye on a pair of shocking electric blue chairs.

Decorating Magazines

Another way you can start to find your personal style is by looking through decorating magazines. They are a great source for ideas. However, looking at these perfect rooms can be intimidating. Stay focused. Look not only for rooms that appeal to you, but for those that have a similar size and structure to your own. In each picture, look for a mood — whether it be casual, formal, country or eclectic — and pick only the ones that are right for you. Get your scissors and start clipping.

If you want to be more specific and only look through the magazines for sofas, for instance, then only look at sofas. Cut out pictures of all the sofas you are drawn to. Don't look at the surroundings. It doesn't matter. Just look at that sofa. Do the same thing for table lamps or whatever the specifics are that you're looking for.

Once you have all your clippings, find the common elements that are so appealing to you. It could be the shape of a leg on a table, the color of woods or the mood in the rooms. Identifying the common ground will help you find your personal style. Maybe even write a list of these characteristics so you'll really understand what you like. Just remember to remain focused and you won't be overwhelmed by all the images.

Compromise

You might think your personal style is one thing, but if you're married or have a roommate and their personal style is something else, it doesn't mean your style has to change. You may not be able to do exactly what you want everywhere, but you can still have a special area in your home for yourself — that's where compromise comes in. Perhaps in the main areas of your home where you spend the most time you could choose the look together. Then, in another room — your bedroom, perhaps — your mate compromises and understands that you're going to do it, say, all romantic, because you're a romantic person. And then in his (or her) office space or den, he wants a modern look. Then you have to understand that it's his space and you can't go in and start placing frills and pillows all about.

No matter what kind of relationship you're in, whether it's a loved one or a roommate, the best thing you can do is stop arguing and being so persistent and start listening. Once you start doing that, the other person will appreciate your ideas even more and you'll create a better living environment.

designer**guy** secret / CHRIS

I'm not very good at compromising, especially when it comes to interior design. It's a very difficult thing for me to do. But I also recognize that if I don't compromise, the space doesn't get pushed to a more creative level because I just want to stop at my ideas. When I finally stop fighting and start listening, a better product is created that makes two people happy. And if I do get my way, it doesn't mean the outcome is going to be good. It could be beautiful, but if my mate is unhappy, what kind of environment have I created for the relationship?

Being Decorators

When we walk into someone's home, we walk in, not to criticize, but to offer a fresh set of eyes. We interview the homeowner to find out exactly what she (or he) likes and doesn't like about her space. Often she loves things that aren't necessarily following rules of décor. For instance, she might tell us that she loves a chair that sits in the corner. We might think that's the worst place for the chair because it doesn't look good, but we work around it: she loves that chair in the corner because

she loves to look at the view from the window. The chair may not be working in the room as to rules and regulations of décor, but if she's enjoying the view, then that is more important than our moving it. It might look more beautiful somewhere else in the room, but she's not going to get any enjoyment out of it. So it's back to lifestyle. It's how you live in your space.

Five Rules of Confidence

1. Never apologize for who you are.

2. Be true to your lifestyle and have confidence in who you are.

3. Change is good. Your style should change as you mature and grow. Your home is the arena for your personal life to be played out.

4. Don't decorate for your neighbors or try to keep up with the Joneses. Who is Mrs. Jones anyway? And why are we trying to impress her?

5. Do what gives you pleasure. Don't allow yourself to be dictated by rules of decorating. Nobody can tell you what gives you pleasure. You have to look at your room and get joy out of it or forget it.

Chris and Steven's Top 10 Decorating Tips

1 Be true to your space, especially its size. If your space is small, embrace it; love it for what it is. Don't try to make it something it isn't. You can try to make it look bigger by painting the whole room white, but it's not going to be bigger. Play up the fact that it's small. If you want a cozy room, paint it a deep rich red. Instead of lots of furniture, get one big sofa or four club chairs. You can still be true to the room's size and use larger pieces of furniture, just fewer of them.

2 Do not be afraid of color. Remember it's only paint. If it doesn't work, paint over it. Start with a quart of paint first and try it on a large piece of board or cardboard. Live with it for a bit and see if you like it. The color will change in different lighting conditions, so look at it in both daylight and at night when you've turned on your lamps.

Be careful when selecting whites. There are many shades of white and lighting will further affect the color. Incandescent light gives a yellow glow. Fluorescent bulbs make things appear blue. Halogen bulbs are the closest to natural lighting. Also consider the effects of the season (see #3 below).

Remember to hold the sample paint color parallel with the wall. Never select a color by looking down at it or in the palm of your hand because light will bounce off the color differently.

3 Think about the seasons when you're choosing color. Keep in mind your surroundings outside when choosing colors for inside, especially paler ones such as whites. A big green tree in your front window is going to cast a green shadow inside. We once painted a turret in a client's house in winter in a creamy stone color. In the summer, she called to complain that the walls of the turret were pink. When we returned we saw that she had a huge red Japanese maple in full bloom. When light came through the window, it reflected off the red leaves and cast a pink hue onto the walls.

4 "Monochromatic" does not have to be taken literally. Monochromatic is generally a single hue in a wide range of values and shades within one color. The best way to give life to a monochromatic space is by using texture. You can use the same color of fabrics, but use different types of weaves, silk, wool and rattan to interject life into a monochromatic space. If you're really daring, add some excitement and throw in a vibrant-colored pillow or other accessory to offset the overall tone.

5 Avoid spending a lot of money on trends. Just like in fashion, decorating trends are ephemeral. They come and go quickly and you'll likely tire of them quickly, too. You can have the latest look by using accessories or other small inexpensive purchases.

6 Invest in simple, but good, tools. Here are five we couldn't live without.
Tape measure Good measurements are essential. Tape measures are now available in everything from metric to imperial to digital readouts.
Small level Instead of arguing with your partner whether something is level, just place it on top of

whatever needs to be checked. It's great for hanging pictures and leveling bookcases.

Low-tack masking tape Perfect for taping off areas when you're painting because it won't peel paint off the wall. We also love to use it for taping out furniture placement on the floors. Don't use regular masking tape because it may peel the varnish.

Foam applicator brushes Keep several of these inexpensive brushes available. They are wonderful for quick touch-ups, and when you're done, just throw them away.

Graph paper Fantastic for mapping out your room. One foot can equal one square, so you can make "to scale" drawings. For instance, if you're thinking of purchasing a six-foot sofa, just count six squares and draw in the sofa. You will know exactly if the sofa will fit on the wall. You will have your own blueprint of your space that you can take shopping with you.

7 It is not a crime to paint wood, well, unless it's some fabulous antique. Some of the old trim in houses, for instance, is inexpensive gumwood.

You don't have to paint all the wood, either. But if you start with baseboards in one room, for instance, continue throughout the house and include the frame around doors and the mantelpiece. This will make the house "flow" because it is a common element that ties each room together. Leave the stairs, railing and floors unpainted, if you want.

Paint also gives new life to old wooden dressers and other furniture. To add a sense of whimsy or something unexpected, paint a garage sale chair bright red or lime green. Several coats of high-gloss paint is an inexpensive way to change your look throughout the seasons.

8 Sometimes good design is more about subtraction than addition. People generally tend to fill their rooms with furniture. Editing is not just about taking things out, but also about grouping, organizing and finding common threads.

The first thing to do when editing is to make an assessment of the room. Usually a few things will have to go because there's just too much in it. You're not able to walk around. Functionally, it's just not working. You have to get rid of some things. Ask yourself: "What is important to me and what isn't." And then be brutal.

When editing a room, don't take away one little piece at a time. It is best to clear the room completely first. Then bring back only those pieces that are necessary for the room or ones with sentimental value. That's a great rule of editing. You can't just take away a lamp and think it's done.

9 Plants are a great way to enhance a space, but they can also overwhelm it. It's more effective if you limit your choice of plants to just a few different varieties and keep the pots in a similar style.

When purchasing trees for the indoors, make sure they come just shy of the ceiling so you accentuate the ceiling's height. Most people purchase a five-foot tree, but have nine-foot ceilings, so the plant looks insignificant. If your plant is small, then think of planting it in a tall urn.

Within reason, try to make your plants fit the theme or style of the room. For instance, ferns or hydrangeas are a good casual plant for the French Country look. Topiaries work in a traditional space. For an eclectic or contemporary look, use tropical plants. For a hard-edge loft, don't use overflowing ferns, but something more graphic or tropical, such as a cactus or palm tree.

10 Organization is one of the biggest challenges for everyone. It doesn't matter how beautiful your space is — if it's not organized, then it's not functional.

The Family

Mother of Style

LIZA WANTS HER home to have a stylish interior, while still serving her family's needs, especially those of her two-year-old son, Liam. Her living room needs some help. It's especially not child-friendly with lamps on top of speakers and cords dangling everywhere. We take it from bland and boring and cluttered to pulled-together and smart and inviting.

We visit a store for all the accessories to spruce up her home, give some older furniture a facelift with fabrics that are beautiful and not off limits to children. We look for sturdy baskets that will hide a multitude of sins and an elegant, but not fussy, mirror to replace the oversized one on the mantelpiece. A huge red Chinese chest that dominates one wall needs particular attention. We'll learn what it takes to create durable style and prove that durable style is not an oxymoron.

"I love the shape of the sofa, but I tell you, I could have this thing dry cleaned every second day. With a toddler, it's just not working. It's not practical."

Liza's Wish List

child-friendly décor • mix of contemporary
and old • stylish interior

Liza's living room is not very friendly to the latest addition to her family — her toddler, Liam. Since having Liam, things that used to matter to her don't as much any more — well, except for her grandmother's heirloom silver and her collection of antiquarian books that she loves. Liza is a real collector, but she has things placed haphazardly around the room. It needs to be tidied up and a place found for all her cherished possessions.

When we first entered Liza's living room, we were struck by what a beautiful bright room it was, but our design focus wasn't clear at the beginning. The room didn't need to be brighter, because there was already a lot of light, plus the walls were painted white. But it needed to be warmer, with a lot of added color — specifically requested by Liza. How to tie it all together? Decorate it so it was child-friendly, but still had some style for the new parents.

BEFORE

Wicker baskets create storage for Liam's toys and comfy machine-washable slipcovers protect the sofa and chair from sticky hands. A lush plant placed on one side of the room balances the huge red Chinese chest that had previously dominated the wall, making the room asymmetrical. A floral arrangement of botanical prints above the sofa gives weight to the wall and balances the fireplace opposite.

27

STEVEN: We're decorating for our youngest client — two-year-old Liam.

CHRIS: We should crawl around on the ground and see what he sees.

To decorate with children in mind, we got down on all fours to experience things from their vantage point. And boy, do the safety issues jump out at you — little hands can grasp so much.

The biggest safety concern was a multitude of lighting cords and dangling wires that were not only hazardous for the lamps, but little Liam as well. Instead of using table lamps, we used wall-mounted lights. The cord is enclosed, so there's nothing for Liam to grab, and any excess cord is tucked away behind the sofa out of harm's way.

Lamps placed on stereo speakers that flanked the fireplace looked like they could topple any moment. We placed three floating shelves on either side of the fireplace to add balance and a place for collectibles that Liza loves to have around her. We painted them the same color as the fireplace and added some decorative trim molding to make them look more traditional.

Lamps precariously balanced on stereo speakers were an accident waiting to happen as were other bric-a-brac around the room (above). High-mounted floating shelves safely show off Liza's collectibles (right). An ottoman covered in the same washable fabric as the sofa creates additional seating.

A large red Oriental chest that housed liquor and the stereo dominated the same wall as the sofa, making the area completely lack symmetry. We needed something substantial to balance the magnificent chest and finally settled on a large tree that added as much impact.

The selling feature of the room was the show-stopping wall of magnificent windows that lead out to the garden. Because privacy wasn't an issue, Liza didn't want to cover them up, but we felt that they were just too overwhelming when you entered the room. Simple sheer curtains with big grommets threaded onto a rod added a contemporary touch and softened the room, but at the same time allowed light through and, most important, didn't block the view.

Seating was an issue, especially for entertaining. We had to think of a way to squeeze in more furniture without overcrowding the room. We didn't want to add more chairs, so instead we slipcovered an ottoman in the same fabric as the sofa. Perfect for comfortable seating and it doesn't block the flow.

The living room is a fantastic bright room that Liza originally painted in a cream color when she first moved in and furnished with a white sofa and chairs. It was suitable for years until Liam came along with his chocolate-covered little hands and then it just didn't make sense any more.

We painted the living room walls the same warm yellow as the dining room to unify the two rooms in the open-concept space. We covered the sofa and ottoman with warm yellow slipcovers. They feel like suede, but they're a machine-washable brushed cotton. For a playful note, we piled the sofa with cushions in stripes, plaids and florals in luscious reds and yellows. Natural wicker baskets and a jute carpet add more warmth to the room.

Color Story

warm yellow

jute

white

red accents

Treasured books and a flouncy fern top the Oriental chest with panache. The wall-mounted lamp provides stylish task lighting, its electrical cord safely stored behind brass tubing.

31

We wanted to bring a burst of color into Liza's dining room, so we had classic cameo chairs reupholstered in art. Really. The chairs were upholstered in artist's canvas, then primed four times, painted in bright vivid patterns and colors and varnished five times. They're one-of-kind, three-dimensional sculpture, and yet they're very functional.

The same warm yellow paint brightens the walls of the living and dining rooms in Liza's open-concept space. Liza specifically requested color: she gets a burst of it in the dining chairs, reupholstered in artist's canvas and hand-painted in unique patterns. They're functional and they sure do brighten up the room.

designer**guys** SECRETS

Kids and Decorating

We wanted to create spaces that had caché for adults but were still comfortable for the kids. Kid-friendly should be adult-friendly, too, and vice versa. There are many choices you can make that will allow kids to have free rein in your homes without giving you a coronary. Do kids and style go hand and hand? We think so!

● Involve your kids in the decorating process. They live there too! If they're old enough, they'll tell you their likes and dislikes, especially when it comes to decorating their bedrooms.

● Baskets with removable lids (no hinges that little fingers can get snagged in) are great for easy, fast storage. Look for something substantial and sturdy, but not too large or too small. Placed on either side of a fireplace, they not only add symmetry, but one can house toys, the other can hold wood.

● Electrical cords and kids don't mix, but rooms need to be lit. Instead of using table lamps, mount wall lights. If you don't want to go to the expense of hiring an electrician to install electric boxes and feed the electrical wire through the walls behind the drywall, look for wall fixtures that have matching tubes, which attach to the walls and direct the wire down to the electrical outlet where you plug it in. The cord is enclosed, so there's nothing for little hands to grab, and any excess cord can be tucked behind a sofa out of harm's way.

● Floating shelves placed high enough are a

great place for collectibles. The shelves are easily mounted by sliding into brackets that are secured to the wall. Put valuable and breakable stuff high up and out of kids' reach.

● Many of us think of primary colors such as bright reds and blues when decorating for children. That's what we thought until we visited a daycare center and were told that muted colors and softer, soothing shades in earth tones were much better for children than vibrant ones, as primary colors were often over-stimulating for most kids. Paint the walls with a semigloss or gloss finish to make cleanup of little finger marks, crayon lines and peanut butter easier. Paints with a flat finish are harder to keep clean.

● Machine-washable slipcovers are a great investment. Fabrics come in a variety of choices from 100 percent cotton to brushed velvet to Ultrasuede®, a synthetic material that feels and looks just like suede. Make sure the fabric is prewashed first before manufactured into slipcovers or pillows to avoid shrinkage in subsequent washings.

● Look for furnishings with soft rounded edges – no hard edges or sharp corners. Round tables soften the look. And glass tables are probably not a good idea in kiddy households.

● Avoid tables with fold-down sides or anything with hinges or hinged lids that can pinch little fingers.

● Watch out for splinters and uneven floorboards on bare wood floors.

Child-Safe Furnishings

Durability is the key word when it comes to designing furniture that kids will be jumping and playing on. Look for furniture that uses screws instead of staples, no-snag springs and web-and-coil construction on upholstered seating, which will be stronger and last a lot longer.

The inner makeup of a good piece of upholstered furniture includes a layer of cotton felt over the wood or springs, then foam and Dacron™. When it's topped with a really durable fabric, you'll have a soft, but firm piece.

Liza's Conclusion

"What I love about it is the feeling of sinfulness and luxury that I feel I shouldn't have if I have a toddler, and yet somehow, miraculously, it's practical."

Inside Out

INSIDE AND OUT, this young family wants an infusion of urban chic into their lives. We treat Sue and Tim's family room and backyard deck as one and give both areas an update from country to modern and turn folksy into fabulous.

It isn't smooth decorating all the way, though. Sue has to convince Tim that they need a change. He isn't so sure. He hates change. In the end, they compromise and with our help get the look they want. We still manage to keep several pieces that they adore and update the look without losing the warmth in the family room that Tim loves.

We ditch the plastic outdoor patio set, find rattan furnishings that work both on the deck and in the family room, slipcover the plaid furniture and install a backyard play area for all the children's toys. Sue just purchased a huge contemporary piece of artwork that isn't working in the cottage-like décor, so we make sure it feels at home, too.

"There are two little guys in here every day — running around and making it a bit dirty. Four years ago we redecorated and it now feels a little old and tired. We're ready for something a little more modern."

Sue and Tim's Wish List

contemporary comfort • keep each other happy • bring indoors out • child-friendly

Our goal is to give Sue and Tim's space a contemporary fresh new look that connects the indoors with the outdoors. An incredible wall of mullioned windows at the back of the house ties the two rooms together. When you're inside, you can see everything outside, and vice versa. We argued over whether to add a window treatment or not. In the end, because privacy isn't an issue, we decided the windows are too beautiful to cover.

BEFORE

Sue and Tim's family room had been updated about four years ago, but now it felt a little tired and country. Sue was ready for something a little more modern and chic. Tim really liked the room and didn't want to change how warm and inviting the room felt. There were pieces that they loved and wanted to keep — the armoire that Sue's father gave them and the coffee table that was a wedding gift. The plaid and dated furniture could all go or be recovered.

Wicker, red pillows and paper lanterns transform the deck. Gone are the plastic furniture and wobbly umbrella (above). Instead, lots of cushions and comfortable seating are the order of the day — perfect for dinner and cocktails outdoors. An oversized market umbrella protects everyone from the sun, while the fabrics are specially manufactured to endure anything Mother Nature sends their way.

CHRIS: Do kids have to have such bright toys?

STEVEN: I guess you want a monochromatic baby too!

Updating the indoors and out with a similar look was proving to be a tough task. And when the going gets tough, the tough go shopping. To create a feeling of unity between the interior and exterior space, we needed to find decorating elements and high-fashion fabrics with durability that would work indoors and out.

We wanted outdoor chairs that didn't look like outdoor chairs and found lacquered wicker chairs meant for indoors that weren't too formal. We knew they would look great outside and could be brought indoors as well when more seating was needed or when the weather turned bad.

We had cushions made for the great outdoor benches Tim made, and slipcovered them in outdoor fabric that resists rain and soiling. We didn't want to give Sue and Tim a standard patio set, so instead we custom-made a square wood table and stained it in a dark chocolate to reflect the coffee table inside. We also drilled a hole in the center to hold a black umbrella. The addition of the wicker chairs completes the furniture on the patio without looking like, well, patio furniture.

A shed was out of the budget for this season, so for a great, quick fix-up we built a secondary fence inside the main fence for all the children's toys to hide behind. It's easy for the kids to access and eventually could be turned into a neat little fort.

Chris, Steven and friend go off to play (left). The same elegance you would expect indoors makes it out to dinner (right). Fine cutlery, a stylish dinner arrangement and floral centerpiece create an outdoor elegance that makes dining alfresco as enjoyable as indoors. Don't forget the wine!

BEFORE

An eclectic mix of furnishings — pared down so each piece gets show-off time — updates Sue and Tim's family room. The whimsical plane on top of the armoire attracts attention and adds a playful note to the room; the basket-weave pattern carpet ties the room together.

We wanted the family room and the patio to have an uninterrupted flow and feel connected, so we stained the deck a dark chocolate just like the floors in the family room. That way when the doors are wide open, it looks like one large room.

We recovered the plaid chairs in the family room in a red fabric and placed matching red cushions on the newly slipcovered gray sofa. Similar red cushions decorate the lacquered wicker armless chairs on the deck.

BEFORE

We carried the wicker theme indoors with a rattan box for the toys, a rope and rattan chair with black cushions, which picks up on the black armoire and black frame of the new painting, and a carpet with a faux basket-weave print. We were worried about Tim, because we knew he didn't like change, but we think he's getting used to it. And the new painting now has a proper room to showcase itself.

Color Story

 gray

 red

 dark chocolate

 natural wicker

 black

A rope and rattan chair is the perfect addition to Sue and Tim's living room. It not only ties in with the outdoor look, but the clean shape gives it a contemporary feel. Hung low on the wall, the art balances the lamp.

designer**guys** SECRETS

Compromising

Sue had to convince Tim that they were ready for a change. Sometimes a little conversation goes a long way to convince a reluctant mate that redecorating is a good thing. Here are some other ways to get the job done:

● Don't be demanding. Gentle persuasion with good backup through pictures and fabric samples is the way to go.

● Listen to what your partner has to say and take his or her suggestions to heart. Don't be so insistent that your ideas are the only ones.

● Pick colors that you both can live with. It may not be your number-one choice, but you have others to consider here.

● Do not monopolize the whole make-over. Let your mate make some decisions, too.

● Do not surprise your partner and make changes without consultation.

● If you have to give in on some big issues, let your personal style shine through in smaller ways, such as cushions, accessories and collectibles.

● Keep some of your mate's favorite items. A comfy chair, for instance, could be recovered in a new contemporary fabric. Think eclectic and match the old with the new.

● Bring in the decorators. Sometimes a third party is just the mediator you need.

Care of Outdoor Furniture and Cushions

There are so many fabrics and natural woods on the market now made especially for outdoor furniture that we hope never to see another plastic chair again.

The choice of colors, textures, patterns and materials are almost unlimited. You can find fabrics from machine-washable to stain-resistant. Most outdoor fabrics are manufactured with an ultraviolet inhibitor to resist yellowing, and cushions are often filled with special non-absorbent polyester filling and a fungicide to deter mold and mildew. However, dirt, dust and suntan oils can still encourage mildew, so proper cleaning on a regular basis is advised.

Furniture

Although we chose indoor wicker chairs to use outdoors for Sue and Tim's deck, it's best to look for all-weather wicker for the great outdoors. Unlike indoor wicker, all-weather outdoor wicker is made of a special very durable resin woven around an aluminum frame. All outdoor furniture should be stored inside during winter to avoid unnecessary weather damage. (For other outdoor furniture suggestions, see *Moving Out*, page 88.)

Wipe up spills and bird droppings with an absorbent cloth as quickly as possible. Vacuum or use a soft brush on wicker and cushions to remove food. Wash briskly with a sponge dipped in mild detergent, such as dishwashing liquid, and warm water to remove soil. Rinse and let dry thoroughly before use.

Cushions

Cover cushions with a towel if you're wearing suntan lotion. The fabric and suntan lotion mixed with the sun's ultraviolet rays cause a chemical reaction that will stain the fabric.

Follow the manufacturer's instructions for fabric care. Generally, most outdoor fabrics are color-fast, but it's still best to test a small hidden area for color-fastness before using any cleaning solution. Scrub cushions with non-abrasive detergent or mild, warm, soapy water. Rinse and let dry before use. If excessive water accumulates in cushions because of washing or rain, stand them upright with zipper or seam-side down.

Painted Finishes

If wicker or other outdoor furniture becomes worn, scratched or chipped, lightly sand the problem area with fine-grit sandpaper. Clean and dry, then touch up with spray paint or stain in the same color.

To paint metal, use products especially designed for that surface. They are rust-resistant and can withstand the elements outdoors.

designer**guys** SECRETS

Staining Decks

For Sue and Tim's deck, we used a dark chocolate translucent stain to maintain the look and feel of wood that Tim loved.

There are three basic stains in a multitude of colors to choose from:

Solid stain or *opaque stain* completely covers the grain and knots of wood and gives it a painted look without the peeling and chipping you often get with a painted exterior. We used an opaque stain on Jamie's deck (see page 85).

Transparent or *translucent stain* shows the grain and keeps the integrity of the look and feel of wood.

Semitransparent stain covers the middle ground. It somewhat covers the wood grain and you can still see and feel the wood, but not as much as with a transparent stain.

Wood should be dry for at least two weeks before staining. Painted wood can't be stained. Before staining furniture, sand slightly with very fine grain sandpaper so you don't scratch the surface and then apply several coats of stain. Let it completely dry before using.

Sue and Tim's Conclusion

"We feel more comfortable in the room now because it reflects our style – the little touches of playfulness and the nice clean feel. So much of what was done seems obvious now – it was so simple, but a smart solution."

SECTION 2

The Entertainers

Gentleman's Quarters

IT'S HARD TO imagine Bernie with a decorating dilemma. He has very good taste and a great knowledge of fabrics and what goes well together. But he does have a few quandaries. One of them being that he feels like he lives in a "big beige box." He needs help turning his overly English traditional home into his dream space.

We come to his rescue and reupholster, reshape, rearrange and reduce in a massive make-over. We look for the perfect fabrics that add a more modern touch. We update his furniture and hunt for that special coffee table with just the right mix of contemporary and traditional. Finally, we turn his fireplace, which looks more like a pizza oven, into the focal point it deserves to be. And, maybe, just maybe, add a hint of color into the beige.

"I like to use the space for entertaining, so we have dinner and then move into the living room for a coffee."

Bernie's Wish List

loves to entertain • update living/dining rooms • clutter-free look • neutral color palette • add a hint of color

BEFORE

Overstuffed furniture and outmoded fabrics can really date a room (left). Streamlined shapes and an updated fabric move the room up to a more modern level. The dark wooden legs of the chairs, taking their cue from the fireplace, add punch to the otherwise monochromatic color scheme.

The furniture in Bernie's home is very traditional, mostly because of his fabric choices, but also because of its shapes. It's good quality, but dated. Here's the perfect place for a little mixing and matching of contemporary with antiques. He wants to keep the integrity of his traditional home, but wants it updated with a hit of modern, as his tastes move toward a more contemporary, urban feel.

Bernie loves to entertain, but right now there's no real flow from the dining room, where he holds numerous dinner parties, to the living room. The angled furniture arrangement makes his large room feel cramped and unfriendly for post-dinner chitchat. We address balancing and integrating both rooms into the mix.

The working fireplace without a mantelpiece in the living room was totally overshadowed by a built-in bookcase filled with books and collectibles. We solved this problem by framing the fireplace with a veneer and staining it with a rich dark chocolate stain. Now, when you first walk into the room, your eye is drawn immediately to it. We simplified the bookcase by installing glass shelves and halogen lighting. It's the perfect place to showcase art and collectibles.

The strength of the fireplace now meant we had to make sure the rest of the room wasn't overpowered and that it also maintained a masculine sense. For balance, we needed something just as dramatic for the opposite wall and shopped for a huge abstract painting. A large piece of artwork is usually more effective than a gathering of many smaller framed pieces.

Finding just the right coffee table for Bernie wasn't an easy task. It almost had to be a piece of art in its own right, because all the other furnishings in the room were so simple. Finally, we found one with a mix of modern glass and wood exactly the same finish as the fireplace. The coffee table has a built-in magazine rack for storage and chrome legs, which add a little more modern into the room.

BEFORE

Originally, the bookcase dominated the living room (left) and overshadowed the fireplace. Not anymore! Boxed-in, veneered and stained a rich dark chocolate, the fireplace is now the focal point, attracting your eye as soon as you walk into the room. And the bookcase? Pared down and refitted with glass shelves and lighting, it's a stunning spot for showcasing select treasures.

STEVEN: Don't be afraid of color.

CHRIS: No, don't go into the color light. Stay over here with me with the beige.

STEVEN: Christopher is King of Monochromatic.

Fabrics were the best place to add color and texture in Bernie's pad. We found Ultrasuede® and heavy velvets in rich browns for the sofa and window coverings. We added brushed cottons and leather. The sleek, simple parson's table in ebony matches the veneered fireplace. We covered the dining chairs in taupe Ultrasuede® and found a contemporary white globe light fixture for above the antique dining table.

Bernie's area rugs in the dining and living room were in perfect shape and were the same color as the newly recovered chairs, but the living room carpet was just a little too large. We cut it down and added a black decorative binding to both area rugs that not only was a nice detail, but also helped define each space.

There's now an overall sense of flow in both rooms — they "read" as one large room. And miraculously they appear larger. Decorating is not always about how something looks, but how it feels as well. We've managed to join these two in Bernie's home — it looks great and feels great, too.

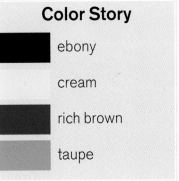

Color Story

⬛	ebony
⬜	cream
⬛	rich brown
⬛	taupe

*A traditional dining room table (right) gets an update with the addition of streamlined
chairs, a contemporary globe chandelier and modern abstract bowl filled with moss, which
adds some softness to the otherwise hard-edged room. This mix of modern with the
old adds a great push-and-pull effect. A large mirror propped against the wall and
flanked by a pair of contemporary sconces (above) reinforces the dynamics.*

designer**guys** SECRETS

Fabrics

Neutrals

Bernie wants a neutral tone-on-tone look with splashes of color. Neutrals are colors that work very well with almost every other color. The standard neutrals are black, beige, white and gray. A neutral doesn't necessarily mean solid, non-patterned or plain. Something neutral could still include a tone-on-tone pattern.

Neutrals are a good way to add design elements without overwhelming the room with color. There are also new neutrals with a more fashion-forward look, such as chocolate brown.

Textures

The key when working with a neutral palette is to mix fabrics of different textures – use silks with velvets, woven fabrics with high pile, chenille with herringbones. Even though the fabric is a solid color, it can still have texture, so there is movement and action within the fabric. Velvets are always a nice touch. Leather adds a masculine note.

Embellishments

You can punch up fabrics and help define them by adding buttons, beaded or wood tassels, fabric or beaded piping, and a variety of different stitching techniques. Baseball stitching is a very simple masculine stitch to add to pillows, draperies and upholstery. Its name comes, obviously, from the stitching on baseballs, which have a double stitch visible on either side of the seam. Beaded tassels and trims add a more feminine look and work very well with silks and velvet. Tassels made with rocks and woods work well on stronger textures such as leather and produce a casual and masculine look.

Fireplace Mantel

Fireplace mantels are the perfect spot for vases and candlesticks, but Bernie already has a built-in bookcase for his collectibles and the last thing he wanted was any more tchotchkes.

Instead of a mantel for Bernie's fireplace, we built an enclosure. We added a subtle four-inch lip, which frames the hearth and adds definition between the upper and lower portions of the enclosure. Unless you're really handy, this is a good job for a carpenter. The opening was recessed slightly, so we could add a slate gray surround. Tiles would work well, too. You don't need a fabulous quality wood like walnut or anything. We built Bernie's wood surround in inexpensive plywood and glued on veneer mahogany strips. We stained it a dark chocolate and then varnished with a satin finish.

designer**guys** SECRETS

Mixing Old and New

Adding new pieces to your home just like you would to update your wardrobe is a great way to freshen things up. There really are no set rules for mixing and matching. In fact, it's really more about breaking the rules. Here are a few things to keep in mind when blending the generations:

● Think balance when you're mixing old and new. Place something new above the older piece so that the heaviness of the antique piece is lightened by the addition of a brushed chrome or nickel vase or light fixture.

● Don't split the two looks – antiques over here, new modern stuff over there. Think of blending the two.

● Freshen up major antique pieces with accessories placed on top, such as sleek tube lamps on Victorian tables. Chrome and glass will add sparkle.

● It's best to leap a generation and then mix together. So don't mix '70s and '80s. Bumping a generation or two gives you a better look.

● Don't overdo it. An eclectic look is great, but learn to edit. Sometimes good design is more about subtraction than addition.

● Every contemporary space needs something with a sense of history in it to keep the space interesting. Hand-carved primitive sculpture or old urns will add interest in a modern space.

● Think push and pull – integrate opposites. For instance, combine something shiny with something matte. A rough concrete bowl will make a statement on a contemporary glass coffee table.

Bernie's Conclusion

"For me, it's always been about how something feels, not necessarily about how it looks. But the guys have managed to join those two. It looks great and feels great."

Be Our Guest

THERE'S A FINE line between wanting to make things very comfortable for your overnight guests and wanting them to get so happy that they never leave. This is particularly true for relatives!

Jill wants to create the most comfy guest room for her parents who visit on a regular basis and have it feel like a seaside bed and breakfast, because her father loves boats. We talk with a window-treatment expert about how to handle a particular challenge, since one window has a beautiful lake view and the other looks out over a shingled garage roof. We shop for items to pamper guests, give tips about great sheets and turn a big bland bedroom into a cozy guest suite.

"My parents live in Florida six months out of the year. I want them to have a place to stay when they visit that feels like home to them, so that when they come here, it truly is their home away from home."

66

Jill's Wish List

B&B-style guest bedroom • subtle nautical look • comfortable and private • cozy and homey

STEVEN: White was nice when the white thing was in.

CHRIS: What? The white thing never went out. White always works.

BEFORE

A guest bedroom is all about making someone feel at home. In this one, the king-size bed was important, because one of the main visitors, Jill's father, is "not a small person." Strong colors and bold stripes cozy up the large room. The heavy-patterned bedspread (left) is updated to a white cover with a solid blue bedskirt in the same fabric as the window coverings (right).

Jill's bedroom is huge. She wants it to be the ultimate welcoming guest room, but right now it's really cold. The stark white walls don't help. The heavy-patterned bedspread and round headboard had their time, but need to be replaced. But it's the windows that present the biggest challenge.

Jill's previous window treatments are just not working. One window has California shutters to block out the awful view and houses across the way that can see right into the bedroom; the other — the one that offers the fabulous view of the lake and pool — has outdated swagged draperies. This is a big feature of the room that we don't want to obstruct. We decided to take both window treatments down and start over.

We've used two layers of floor-length window coverings: sheers next to the glass and deep royal blue cotton on a separate rod over that. Both can be pulled for various degrees of privacy or opened to reveal the view. To unify the two windows, we attached matching fabric-covered valance tops to both.

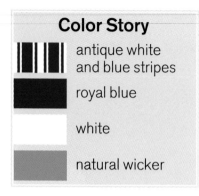

Color Story

- antique white and blue stripes
- royal blue
- white
- natural wicker

The bedroom is a huge room with no architectural details. We knew we had to activate it in some way, so to punch up the walls we chose an antique white and blue tent stripe wallpaper — so called because if you're daring enough to run it across the ceiling, it makes the room look like a tent. Tent stripes work really well in a big room. It's a pattern that helps to liven up the room and creates a little bit of an illusion that the walls are higher.

The wallpaper is very intense and powerful. We didn't want the room to get too busy, so we've used neutral fabrics throughout in the same colors as the wallpaper.

We wanted Jill's room to have a real casual elegance. Black-and-white photographs of boats add an understated nautical theme. A classic wingbacked chair upholstered in a soft seagrass, and natural wicker and bamboo side tables are all appropriate touches for a seaside B&B.

BEFORE

Jill's beautiful antique armoire housed a TV but was placed in an odd position in the room (left), making television viewing difficult. She wanted to keep it, so we moved it across from the bed. Now it's not just a piece against the wall, but a functioning and beautiful part of the room (right).

Jill wanted a seating arrangement by the window overlooking the lake and pool where her guests could enjoy a morning coffee and drink in the view. Unfortunately, that meant her comfy chaise lounge that was only suitable for one had to go. Instead, we placed a simple adjustable metal table by the window, flanked by two cane chairs we brought up from the basement. Painted and recovered with royal blue cushions and white piping, they became perfect found treasures.

To accentuate the king-size bed, we custom-made a five-foot-tall white padded square headboard to replace the rounded one. Then we made a blue covering that attaches onto the headboard with Velcro™ that can be easily removed, washed and then put back on.

The fabric on the bed is white with a solid blue bedskirt in the same fabric as the window coverings, which adds a nice calming feeling in the room and anchors the furniture against the vibrant stripes.

Padded headboards are great in guest rooms, or any room really, because they muffle sound. You often find padded headboards, especially tall ones, in luxury hotels, so when you're sleeping you won't be disturbed by noise from another room. They also provide comfort for sitting up in bed and reading a book or watching TV.

designer**guys** SECRETS

Suite Dreams

The best way to make your guests feel right at home is to pamper them with luxury. When your guests arrive, they may have traveled for a very long time. Make sure they have everything they need. They may have forgotten to bring certain things, so have them all ready for them and they won't have to ask. Little touches of home are invaluable in making a guest feel welcome.

● Fill decorative baskets with soaps, bath bombs, bath gel, toothbrushes, toothpaste, hand lotion, shampoos, combs, headache pills, candles and other "home away from home" items.

● Provide a hair dryer.

● Place hand and face towels nearby. Hang bath towels near the tub or shower.

● Provide a personal pair of disposable slippers.

● The ultimate in luxury, and something your guest probably wouldn't travel with because it's so heavy and bulky, is a comfy terry-cloth bathrobe for use while visiting.

● If guests have traveled far to stay with you, provide an assortment of local postcards and stamps for them to send back home. A city map could also be useful to them as they make their way around.

● Find out what interests your guest and place books and magazines on these subjects by the bed. Make sure a lamp is nearby for easier reading. Bottled water and glasses add a thoughtful touch, as does a small dish of mints or sugar-coated almonds.

● Plug a night-light into a wall socket to light the way to the bathroom.

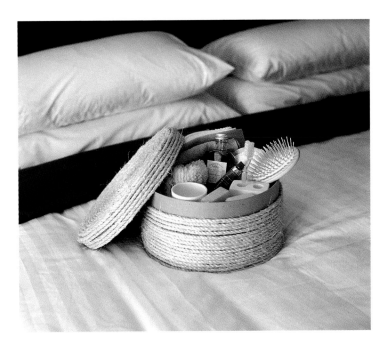

designer**guys** SECRETS

Making Your Bed
Great Sheets

When you think that we spend upwards of eight hours or more in our beds, it's really important to be comfortable, and nothing beats a quality sheet. Your guests will love you for it.

One hundred percent cotton sheets are by far the nicest. Cotton is valued for its soft and breathable nature. Many brands are now wrinkle-free and require no ironing. Cotton/polyester blends on the other hand offer the benefit of non-wrinkling, but don't feel as nice as pure cotton. They also have a tendency to pill — those little balls of thread that often appear on sheets and are so uncomfortable to sleep on — and lose their vibrant colors and feel sweaty in summer and clammy in winter.

Other popular sheet fabrics include flannel, knitted jersey and sateen, which feels slippery.

Thread Count

Thread count is the measure of how many threads are woven into one square inch of fabric. Generally, the higher the thread count, the smoother and softer the sheet. Two hundred threads per inch used to be the most common luxury weave and the minimum most savvy consumers would buy, but today even higher thread counts are widely available, some over 300 per inch. To get the softest feel, stay around a 250-thread count or higher and avoid any fabrics less than 225. Look for sheets in an all-combed cotton percale – which refers to a tightly woven fabric – and a "Machine Wash" care label. Nobody wants to dry clean sheets.

Pillows

Pillows are so important for a good night's sleep that some people travel with their own. Should they be filled with down, feathers, a mixture of both or foam? It's impossible to guess what your guests might prefer, but you can't go wrong with good quality. Fluff them up and, just in case, have on hand allergen-proof undercovers for allergy sufferers.

Bed Covers

Feather bed covers add a layer of luxury to the mattress. You always want your guests to have a comfortable night's sleep.

Jill's Conclusion

"As soon as I walked in, I just felt warmth, hominess, that bed-and-breakfast feeling that I was looking for. Maybe this will be my room. I can't believe the comfort, the coziness. My parents are never going to leave here."

Totally Exposed

JAMIE'S LOFT PRESENTS an interesting design dilemma. He has a hot deck with a cool view that he hopes to turn into a happening place. The drawback, though, is that both the homeowner and his guests have to pass through the bedroom to get there. It's a definite detraction. When you have a private area that you also want to be a public space, a smooth transition is what you need. We want to separate the two somewhat, but at the same time give each area a similar feel, so that moving from one space to the other is seamless and soothing, rather than sudden and jarring.

On the deck, we choose furnishing and paint finishes that will stand up to any beating the blazing elements of sun, wind and rain might create. We shop for market umbrellas and outdoor accessories, the best plants for using outside and bedroom furniture that makes a statement. At the end of the day, this strong, silent guy has a very cool space to entertain his friends and a very masculine place to lay his head.

"Although the deck and bedroom are separate areas, I want them to have a similar feel, so you don't feel like you're walking through one space and then all of a sudden, boom, you're in a completely different-looking space."

Jamie's Wish List

loves to be outside • entertain on deck • smooth transition from bedroom to deck • shower on deck

STEVEN: Because Jamie is a jock, what if for inspiration we went to a gym?

CHRIS: Well, okay, but how do you decorate a deck to look like a gym?

STEVEN: I don't think it has to be that literal. Most gyms are decorated with a hard edge. You find lots of chrome with black, red, gray carpets. Do you ever see a gym with fluffy white pillows and fake palm trees?

CHRIS: If I went to a gym, that's the kind of gym I'd want to go to!

Jamie's space presented several design challenges. Not only did he want his bedroom to act less like a bedroom, but he also wanted his deck to be more than a deck.

Since the only way to get to the deck is through the master bedroom, the furniture needed to be less personal. We solved the bedroom quandary by choosing furnishings that would have felt more at home in a dining room, such as a dark walnut credenza rather than a traditional dresser for his clothes. The heavy dark bed is very masculine and anchors the room. We created a living room-like seating area, complete with reading materials, and anchored the television to the ceiling similar to an airport waiting room. Lamps, side tables and artwork, in this case, photographs, wouldn't feel out of place in a living room or office space and result in an unbedroom-like look.

We created this lounge-like area (left) opposite Jamie's bed to make the bedroom seem less private for guests passing through en route to the deck. The chairs and a table stacked with reading material make the space look like a doctor's waiting room.

Jamie is a jock and spends much time boxing, so for inspiration we thought of a gym. We found a place for Jamie's boxing gloves (right) that allows them to double as art and be accessible for his left hook.

Jamie's bed is strong on design but does not overwhelm the room (left).
A row of framed prints hung above the bed reflects a similar treatment
on the credenza-turned-bureau (above) which passersby encounter
as they make their way to the deck.

BEFORE

Jamie loves to entertain. On the one hand, he wants his deck to be a place for dinner parties, but he also wants a place for sunbathing and casual get-togethers. So, we create two complementary spaces for him to entertain.

The dining area is defined by an umbrella table and comfy teak chairs. Instead of fighting an enclosure for the air conditioner, we work with it and turn it into a built-in bar tucked into the corner. We provide a clearance around the air conditioner to allow it to function properly before finishing it with a removable tiled top.

Across from the dining area, two low-lying flat lounge chairs with wheels and grass cushions can be moved around to follow the sun. An extra table nearby holds refreshments, bath towels and candles. The *pièce de résistance* is a simple outdoor shower. Now Jamie can have his cake and wash it off, too!

Although we enclosed Jamie's air conditioner (right), it is very important to check with a heating contractor and the building codes in your area for any bylaws before enclosing yours. Outdoor air-conditioning units in most homes have a condenser in them. When the air conditioner is active, this condenser makes a noise and blows air out of the top of the unit. Most of these units need to have at least 18 inches of space open around them; otherwise they could overheat. Never seal a unit up completely.

The view from the deck is unbelievable, especially at night. Since we didn't want anything on the deck to be stronger than the view, we chose huge concrete planters to match the backdrop of the city.

We wanted the transition to be smooth from bedroom to deck, so we picked strong dark masculine colors, such as black and dark chocolate. The bedroom sheets are charcoal gray to blend with the concrete outside.

White cushions and wheat grass mats are accent colors.

For privacy, we added higher boards to the sides of the existing outdoor walls. It gives the deck a clean look and neighbors can't see in. To lighten and brighten the wood on the deck, we used an opaque stain instead of paint, which has the same effect, but is low maintenance and won't chip or peel like paint. We also positioned the outdoor lights along the bottom of the fence to add a wash of light across the floor. Placed higher up, the light would have been too harsh.

Color Story

- concrete
- black
- dark chocolate
- charcoal gray
- taupe
- white
- wheat

We designed oversized concrete planters (left) for Jamie's deck to complement the city in the background. This solution is not appropriate for every deck because of the weight involved. If you are interested in having planters, check with an architect or contractor first — you don't want them falling through the floor. Another effective solution, if you don't have a crane or muscle at your disposable, is to install oversized built-in wooden plant boxes, but again, check with a pro first about the weight-bearing capabilities of your deck. Wood is heavy stuff, too. So is the earth in the planters! Also, make sure there is drainage for water from either rain or hand watering, so the roots don't get waterlogged.

designer**guys** SECRETS

Smooth Transitions

Make a corridor or walkway through the private sleeping area. You can do this by creating an area opposite the bed that has a lounge-like feel with chairs and a table stacked with reading material, similar to a doctor's waiting room.

When shopping for bedroom furnishings, don't limit your selections to traditional bedroom furniture. Think "outside the box." Sometimes dining or living room furniture, such as the walnut credenza we chose for Jamie's dresser, may be appropriate for your bedroom as well (or vice versa).

Place the TV at an elevated level to create an atmosphere less like a bedroom and more like an airport lounge. Wall or ceiling brackets are available at most hardware stores to secure the television.

Choose dark strong colors such as black and chocolate brown to make it less personal.

Keep the design elements simple. Go understated and not jazzed up with a lot of detail. Keep personal items, mementos and family photos to a minimum.

Screens, room dividers, curtains and potted plants also work to separate a private space from a public area or to create a corridor.

Moving Out

Decorate your outdoor space as though it was indoors. Think of the function of the space. Is it a place for eating, entertaining or just relaxing? Try to imagine your guests flowing through and using the area.

Choose weather-friendly furniture able to withstand scorching sun or pelting rain. Some natural materials are ideal for this. Woods, especially teak, can withstand any weather that nature tosses its way. Cedar is also good – strong, durable and rugged, and will stand up to all the elements. Other materials to consider for outdoors are painted or sealed wrought-iron, aluminum and colorful resin tables and chairs.

Teak furniture will naturally weather to a soft silver gray color due to natural oxidation of the wood. To maintain the original wood color, use a teak cleaner, following the instructions on the container. To clean and leave the silver gray color, use mild soap and water. Do not use any type of oil if furniture is used outside. This may cause mildew and irregular coloring.

Outdoor chairs should be as comfortable as indoor ones. Cover them with cushions in outdoor fabrics that just need a light wiping off with a damp cloth. Outdoor fabrics are especially formulated to endure anything Mother Nature can throw at them. Most are water repellant with mildew resistance. Make sure the pillows have zippers, so the shells can be removed and thrown into the wash.

Create a seating area between two planters. Stain-resistant cushions add comfort.

Outdoor Shower

Outdoor showers are a great idea. While sunbathing you can instantly "cool off." It's the next best thing to a swimming pool. They need not be anything elaborate, either. If you've been sunbathing and are covered in suntan lotion, there's no need to traipse through the house making a mess. Just rinse off outside.

An outdoor shower needs a place for runoff of excess water, so a drain and proper plumbing are very important. It is best to consult with a general contractor before starting.

Planting Roots

Containers or big plant boxes are ideal for rooftop decks. Many decks get a lot of sun during the day, so any plant you choose needs to be able to hold up against the elements, including winter. Trees are ideal because they can withstand most environmental conditions and they don't need as much care as flowers. Check with your local garden centers to make sure these shrubs and plants are appropriate for your growing zone. Here's a roundup of the best:

Junipers

The Medora Juniper has a blue tinge to it. It grows from 10 to 12 feet tall, 3 to 4 feet wide. Tolerates heat, cold and drought. Prune it to keep it more compact and the height down. But remember, when you start pruning a plant, you have to keep at it, because the very act of pruning encourages growth.

Skyrocket Juniper

This juniper is a more architectural-looking plant with a column-like shape and the narrowest juniper available. Gets only about 18 to 24 inches wide with a height of 12 feet or so.

Boxwoods

These are excellent plants for containers on the deck. They take very well to training and shaping. A tall column shape will keep its leaves all winter long.

Cedars

Cedars are also good on decks, especially if you don't have full sun. They thrive in sunny to partly shady conditions. The Emerald Cedar grows upright to an average height of 12 feet and is 2 to 3 feet wide.

To complement the boxwood, place a Globe Cedar in front. About 3 feet in diameter, this plant forms a perfect globe without trimming. Little Giant is the compact form with vivid dark green foliage. It is 18 to 24 inches in diameter.

Spartan Juniper

Very bright green plant that loves hot, hot sun. Grows from 10 to 12 feet tall, 3 to 4 feet wide.

Maintenance

Junipers and boxwoods are great outdoor plants that will do fine throughout the winter. For windy areas, such as balconies or rooftops, place a bit of screen over them during the cold months to prevent the wind from contacting the foliage directly. Burlap works very well. Just make sure it doesn't touch the foliage itself.

If there is a lot of wind on the balcony, place crushed stones around the base of the tree. This will help prevent the soil from blowing out of the container. It also adds a clean look. We used white crushed stones in Jamie's planters.

Outdoor plants need to be watered. They cannot survive on rainfall alone. Water according to specific plant's instructions.

Going Out for Dinner

Dining alfresco and entertaining outdoors is perfect for warm-weather get-togethers, but to make it happen easily requires some preliminary attention to details.

● Stylish canvas market umbrellas are very effective in offering protection from the sun and cover a relatively large area without closing off too much light. Shade-creating pergolas made from slats of wood or vine-covered arbors that block out the bulk of the sun's rays but filter the light through in a dappled fashion are also good ideas. Canvas cabanas with flowing cotton draperies are another good idea, but they may feel confining when you're sitting inside them and they'll create a solid "block" on your deck.

● Encourage your guests to relax through leisurely meals by keeping them comfy with all-weather cushions especially fitted to the chairs.

● Create the same elegance you would indoors with linen napkins, a damask-covered table and fine cutlery and wineglasses. Use heavier glassware, however, nothing too delicate, to protect from windy situations.

● Set up an extra table to hold additional refreshments. Candles protected by glass hurricane shades, and a simple floral arrangement, will add a tropical flare.

Jamie's Conclusion

"I'm one happy boy, let me tell you. I've got the sun, I've got the stars, I've got the city. I've got a brand new deck. Perfect! I'm so happy."

Shall We Dine?

RIANNE'S DINING ROOM is the size of her personality. It sets the stage for family dinners of fourteen, but she hasn't redecorated in more than twenty years. The dining room is very dark and very fussy. And although it was well done, we think it's time to brighten things up. Paring down, cleaning up and updating are all on the schedule.

Should the molding around the room stay or go? Should the chandelier come down? The heavy drapes and wallpaper need lightening up for sure. The dining room table and chairs are in perfect condition and a very fine quality, but they're just too dated, so we take them to a faux finisher for a facelift. A dried-flower arrangement may have been popular back then, but needs to be replaced with something fresher and cleaner now. We shop for botanical prints, a new mirror for over the buffet and a lighter window treatment and carpet. We turn dark and dated into light and elegant.

"I've loved my dining room for twenty-four years and I still love it, but it's dark. It's probably the fact that I'm away all winter in a house down south that has a lot of light, and when I come home I feel as if this closes in on me."

92

Rianne's Wish List

update '80s look • lighten up • more casual • less opulent • accommodate a large crowd

STEVEN: Rianne doesn't want her place to look done done.

CHRIS: She just wants it to look done.

When Rianne's dining room was first decorated, she wanted a very elegant, formal look. Asian influences in the wallpaper and drapes and Chinese ginger jars suited her then. Now that she's retired, her lifestyle is a little more casual and she isn't looking for the opulence she was looking for then.

The dining room is very tasteful and well appointed. Somebody had paid attention to the details. It's a challenge for us because it still looks really good. The fabric choices are dating it and the window treatments and wallpaper are very heavy and dark. The lush garden out front is completely obstructed. The chandelier — all crystal and glass — is beautiful but too opulent and overpowering. The carpet is still in great shape, but the colors are reflective of the window treatment and wallpaper. Rianne is open to big suggestions and we're going to give them to her.

BEFORE

Heavy swagged window treatments and an opulent chandelier are reminders that this dining room (left) hadn't had an update since the '80s. A little paint on the table, some new soft fabric for the chairs, a hurricane lamp and silk flowing draperies give the room a fresh new look (right).

As usual we argue over details, but decide to keep the molding on. The moldings offer an opportunity to break up tonality and add a bit of visual interest without being overwhelming. We finally agree to remove the chandelier. There's nothing understated about it, so down it comes.

The previous window coverings were very fussy, with a heavy print and large swag. We want a much simpler look, so we replace them with subtle beige silk and let them hang straight to the floor. The dining room furniture, although still in good shape and very well made, is just a little too dated. We want its color to reflect the beige fabric that we picked for the walls and curtains, so rather than replace it, we give the legs and skirt a subtle antique white faux finish. We reupholster the black moiré chairs in a beige tone-on-tone fabric, and because of the style of chair, we are able to upholster the back panel in a silk fabric that reflects the window treatment we've chosen.

We wanted to find a mirror for the dining room that was a little unusual — something not too stately or formal. We settled on a floor-to-ceiling conservatory-style framed mirror to place at the back of Rianne's antique serving table. We replace the opulent crystal chandelier with a hurricane lamp, which is still a classic and has reflective qualities, but is clear and casual — perfect for the new look we have in mind.

A bright fresh floral arrangement adds an elegant touch to a table setting (right). For other unusual floral arrangements, think of combining rosemary and roses, which smell great together, or make a nest out of branches of willow, birch and dogwood. A floor-to-ceiling conservatory-style mirror (above) sits behind the server. Classic lamps provide mood lighting.

Color Story

beige

antique white

dark chocolate

taupe

leaf green accents

Rianne's dining room walls had been papered in a very heavy dark pattern to match the window treatments with cream-colored molding. This made the walls very busy and we wanted to neutralize them. To do this, we removed the wallpaper and painted the walls and the panel molding in the exact same beige color right up to the crown. When you look around the room now, the panel molding becomes a subtle detail instead of the main focus.

Below the chair rail we applied wallpaper in the same color as the walls. The wall covering has a subtle pattern that gives visual interest to the lower portions of the walls.

We chose fabrics that were in neutral beige. The sisal carpet on the floor is taupe. We added a bit of green to Rianne's dining room with a botanical theme and placed oversized botanical prints on the wall, pressed-leaf candles on the table, a large fern plant in the corner and huge topiaries on either side of the server. The faux-finished skirt and legs of the dining room table are in an antique white glaze with a nice deep chocolate stain on the top.

BEFORE

designer**guys** SECRETS

Updating an '80s Look

The '80s were the glamorous gold-gilt decade. Everything was about extravagance and excess and it was reflected in our decorating. With just a little updating and a whole lot of editing, it's easy to move forward into a more contemporary look without replacing all your furniture. Here's how:

● Editing is a great first step. The '80s was all about lushness and extravagance. Today, the look is much cleaner and streamlined. Update by trimming the excesses and adding a few new touches. The best way to edit a room is to remove all the furniture right down to the bare walls and then bring the pieces back in. But only bring back in what is essential to the room.

● If you don't want to make any new purchases, there are many simple techniques for updating a look. A glitzy gold mirror with an '80s look, for instance, can be modernized with a silver foil treatment, or slipcovers in the latest fabrics can change the look of your furniture.

● Remove heavy dark wallpaper and repaint the walls in a fresh new color.

● Fussier details in a room, such as molding, can still remain. In Rianne's dining room we left it, but painted it the same color as the rest of the walls.

● Make the room feel more casual by your choice of fabric, carpet and drapery. Think natural fabrics such as linen, cotton, silk and sisal.

● Replace the opulence of a huge crystal chandelier with a classic hurricane one or something simpler.

● Replace swagged window treatments with long draperies hung straight to the floor.

● Single- or double-pinch pleat drapery will feel less fussy and full and more streamlined.

● Replace dried floral arrangements with fresh-cut flowers.

Rianne's Conclusion

"Is this the same place? It's so different and it's so light, but it's warm and elegant and very beautiful. It feels very much like home. It is astounding."

The Collectors

Lofty Ambitions

IT'S THE AGE-OLD problem of having too many beloved possessions and not enough room to contain them. Kirsti is a young entrepreneur who moved into her first loft with a treasure trove of past belongings, including some huge furniture that was more appropriate in her larger previous space. The result is not enough room to move around and no clear design focus. Back up the truck because we're turning overcrowded into crowd-pleasing.

We begin by editing out what she doesn't need and then move on to rebuild her surroundings to show off and reflect her Finnish heritage, of which she's very proud. We shop for clean-edge modern furniture of glass, chrome and steel, and ceramic accessories. A window-treatment expert tells us how to get Kirsti her much-needed privacy and we create a special wall of art.

"I'm not using the living area between the kitchen and the stairs because I find I'm always dodging furniture."

104

Kirsti's Wish List

make the place more functional • privacy • reflect heritage • simple clean lines

BEFORE

Square footage is at a premium in this loft, so the furniture choices had to be well appointed. Overstuffed furniture from a previous life (left) had to go. Cool vinyl recovers the heirloom chairs and a slender blue armless sofa hits the right notes (right). The only place to get real estate is to go up. Hence the pastel-colored artwork made especially for Kirsti that capitalizes on the loft's height.

Urban living generally means tighter living quarters. It's really a question of space, or lack of space, that we need to address in Kirsti's two-storey loft. Kirsti is not enjoying her furniture from her previous apartment in her new space. We hunt for furniture that is space saving and well appointed and turn the dull into delicious.

We wanted a sofa with a fresh, bright color and streamlined shape. We also wanted it to complement her two Finnish classic chairs. We found the perfect blue armless sofa. It's light and airy, but still feels substantial. Without arms, it won't close in the room, and because the sofa is the first thing you see when you descend the stairs from the upper level, you won't feel like you're bumping into it. A glass "waterfall" coffee table appears to float, white vinyl slipcovers add new life to her favorite heirloom chairs, and the shapes of the tall slim lamps on either side of the sofa are reminiscent of Finnish glass.

SELKEYS TILA

ENERGIA KAUNEUS

TYYLI ONNI

STEVEN: You can never be too tall or too blond.

CHRIS: Well, that's easy for you to say.

STEVEN: I'm talking about the wood and the height of Kirsti's space.

BEFORE

When you have a small space to decorate, it's probably best to use a monochromatic color scheme to make the place look larger, but if followed too closely, it can sometimes be a little too rigid and uptight. In Kirsti's space, we added subtle splashes of color through artwork, pillows, a duvet and, of course, that fabulous blue sofa. We tied the kitchen and living room together by painting the kitchen's backsplash blue to pick up the blue sofa in the living room.

We also wanted to embrace Kirsti's Finnish heritage. We did this not only through glass, but by filling her two-storey wall with artwork created especially for her. We stenciled Finnish words that reminded Kirsti of her background onto six pastel-painted canvasses. The words such as "happiness," "calm" and "confidence" express what she feels in her space.

Now that we've opened up the loft and brought it all together with color, there's a much stronger sense of flow. It doesn't feel as divided anymore.

Color Story

blue

blond wood

white

pastels

The cool new furniture and smart layout make the living area seem twice as large. Balancing the smooth textures of the sofa, chairs and trolley table, a long-hair shag rug ties the room together.

Finland is known for its quality glass, and we wanted to use as much of it as possible in Kirsti's space. Kirsti already has a great collection of Finnish glass from such classic designers as Alvar Aalto and Tapio Wirkkala, whose work is highly prized and very collectible.

The railings that visually cut the space in half were our first challenge. They were also too industrial looking. We decided to replace the interior panels with clear glass for a cleaner look. (see below)

The second challenge was on Kirsti's second floor. She desperately needed a place for storage and a private dressing area. We found a perfect area to install a frosted-glass panel that extends right to the ceiling and lets the light in but keeps prying eyes out.

designer**guys** SECRETS

Window Treatments

Kirsti's two-storey loft has four windows – all huge and all visible at the same time from any given point. One window is in the bedroom, two large windows are stacked on top of each other in the living room and the other is in the kitchen.

If we gave all four windows the same treatment, it would not only be boring, but it would look like giant dice. Since we are working in a two-storey loft, we wanted to play up the height.

Fabric and hardware options are all things to consider. For instance, a giant Roman blind to cover the two huge living room windows is not an option. There isn't a cleat big enough to wind all that excess cord around.

Other things to consider when picking a window treatment are:
- material to use
- location of windows
- exterior light available
- direction the space faces
- is the treatment going to open from left to right, bottom to top, or top to bottom
- is there a need for privacy or is the covering a decorative feature only
- does it reflect your personal style

For the kitchen, we chose a white shimmery material. You can't see through it, but it's good for light filtration. We decided to put the curtains on a Velcro™ track for easy removal and cleaning. It's also a cinch to install: the aluminum track has the Velcro™ attached.

In the living room, we wanted to accentuate the height and give some sense of privacy. The window treatments are two panels of fabric adhered by a Velcro™ strip. They come shooting down all the way from the ceiling to the floor and have little tiebacks for pulling back. When they need dry cleaning, Kirsti can climb up on a ladder and pull the draperies from the Velcro™ track, dry clean them and then put them back up.

In the bedroom, there was a privacy issue and light just spilled in. Kirsti hasn't had a good night's sleep since she moved. There were several options to consider here.

Dim Out is a light cheesecloth fabric that has had a bit of rubber poured over it. It's very thin and keeps light out.

The light in Kirsti's bedroom was so intense that we opted for the next level. Black Out is a non-porous fabric with a charcoal filter. A bit of rubber is poured onto the back and front. It allows no light to penetrate. Don't be put off by the word "black" here. The window treatments and backing come in all colors. Kirsti's are white.

designer**guys** SECRETS

Tips for Decorating a Small Space

In a small space, every inch is valuable. So keep form and color to a minimum. Having correct measurements is really key, especially when shopping for furniture. Draw floor plans marked up with room dimensions and carry this with you when you shop. (Carry fabric swatches and paint chips, too.) Don't forget to measure the opening of the door frames and elevators, if you live in an apartment or loft, to make sure that the sofa you love so much will fit.

Color

Instead of staining cupboard doors, paint them the same color as the walls. This way, when your eye goes around the room, it skips over them. It's a nice detail because the cupboards will just blend right in. In Kirsti's loft, we left the wood blond, because it was just so light and beautiful. Add splashes of color etc.
Add splashes of color through artwork, accessories and pillows.

Furniture

Buy multi-purpose furniture, such as box-like coffee tables and ottomans with lids to store books and magazines. If you have lots of sleepover friends, invest in a good sofa bed rather than a conventional sofa, and you have an instant guest room.

Find an armoire in your personal style that becomes a focal-point piece and stores the TV and books.

Create visual interest with a unique piece of furniture, such as an heirloom or classic chair, ceramic vase or large piece of artwork.

Upholster big pieces of furniture, such as sofas, in solid colors. (Patterned fabric will dominate a room.)

Large mirrors can increase the perceived size of a room and bounce light around effectively.

Floors

Select a simple neutral-colored, textured carpet throughout. Avoid boldly patterned and multicolored carpets and the use of many small area rugs.

When choosing your carpet, make sure you have your fabric samples with you. That way you can ensure you're choosing the exact color. Also, bring a sample of the carpet home with you, so you can see how it works in the lighting conditions in your home.

Storage

Storage in a small space can be a challenge. Select a small area that can be enclosed behind a smoky glass panel that doubles as storage and a dressing area, the way we did for Kirsti.

If your kitchen doesn't have a lot of cupboard space, build in bookcases to hold glasses and dinnerware. Store food items in galvanized containers, which visually tie in with the exposed ductwork that often exists in lofts.

Decorative boxes and wicker baskets are great for storing books and magazines.

Out with the Old

If you have furniture – like Kirsti had – that still has lots of life in it but is just not working for you now, here's what you can do to get rid of it:

- Give it to family or friends who need it.
- Give it to charity for use in their facilities or for sale in their shops. Many will come and pick it up and take it away, but the waiting list for pickup can sometimes be up to two months long, so plan ahead.
- Hold a garage/lawn sale. (Can you schlepp the sofa out?)
- Hold a house sale.
- Advertise the pieces you have for sale in your city or neighborhood newspaper.
- Sell it to a second-hand furniture store. Often these types of stores are looking for antiques. Look in your yellow pages under "Furniture – Used" or "Second-Hand Stores" for someone in your area.
- Sign up with a consignment shop. They're fairly recent players on the used-furniture scene. They do the selling for you. Usually, you agree on the selling price together. Then you divide the receipts – anywhere from a 50/50 split to a 60/40 split. Generally, you get the higher percent. Most consignment shops do not pick up, but they will arrange a mover for you, which you'll have to pay for. If the stuff hasn't sold within a certain time frame, the price will be reduced, and if it still hasn't sold, you can have it back or they will donate it to charity.

Kirsti's Conclusion

"I enjoy the simplicity and functionality of Scandinavian design. I knew when I redid my apartment that that's the direction I wanted to go in, and I think it's been captured perfectly here."

Art Works

JENNIFER BOUGHT THE first house that she looked at. She wanted something that had an open-concept feeling, like a loft. But because she had spent so many years in an apartment, she was really looking forward to having a backyard where she could go outside and relax. She likes the idea of loft living, but she still wants to maintain the hominess of a house. Our mission is to preserve the modern-loft look and finish the space with the comforts of home.

The house has a well-designed main floor, and with Jennifer's choice of stunning colors, modern furniture and art, the place looks great. So what's the problem? The previous homeowner, an architect, had great dreams and goals, but didn't quite finish things off. The wavy and low ceiling makes us feel seasick. Another challenge is the windows that were installed slightly crooked. It's an old house with charm, but at the same time we need to address some of its irregularities. We use paint technique and window treatments to disguise the flaws. We also go shopping for some modern accessories to showcase the beautiful contemporary sofa and chairs designed and made by Jennifer's father and find the perfect dining table and seating. We turn urban cool into cosmo comfort.

"I really was looking forward to having a backyard. But also I wanted something that was quite modern, like a loft, and that I really didn't have to do a lot of work on."

Jennifer's Wish List

give house a loft feel • make different-style furniture work • showcase artwork • keep it homey

BEFORE

Jennifer needs a table in her dining room and something that will go with two great chairs her grandmother left her. The fabric, though, needs a little updating. The window treatment in the dining room was a leftover from the previous owner and certainly isn't reflective of Jennifer. There's an alleyway outside, so she wants to make sure that she gets privacy but still gets some light coming in. Plus you can see both the living room and dining room windows at the same time when you stand in the middle of the dining room, so both treatments have to work together.

The living room is really, really tiny. Her retired father's office furniture looks great, but it's pretty big and bulky, and really tough to maneuver around. We need to reconfigure the layout, so you're not tripping over the furniture. Obviously, the focus in the living room is the working fireplace, but it is slightly off-center, with an air duct on one side.

Between Jennifer's father's modern office furniture and her grandmother's '50s-style chairs and Jennifer's own contemporary art collection, there's definitely a push and pull going on in the rooms. We love it, though, because if it gets too perfect, then you lose some personality and this place has lots of that.

Jennifer's original placement of furniture (above) did not allow for easy accessibility. By reconfiguring the furniture (right), it's now much easier to move around. Two enormous trees in oversized planters placed on either side of the fireplace divert attention from the air duct on one side, which was throwing off the balance.

CHRIS: You don't have to have a back on a dining room chair, do you?

STEVEN: But this choice of yours look like little button ottomans.
I had one of these when I was seven.

For Jennifer's dining table, we picked a strong masculine piece to anchor the room. Her grandmother's chairs at the ends of the table have a retro feel and we didn't want to detract from them, so we chose leather cubes for seating around the table.

Every contemporary space needs one element that doesn't seem to belong. And in Jennifer's case, we selected a hand-carved wooden trough for her dining table. We don't literally expect her guests to eat out of it, but as a display for grass, an arrangement of flowers or a prop against the wall, it's perfect.

While we were doing a second look in the living room, we noticed that the wall on one side of the fireplace stepped out, throwing off the balance. To divert attention from this, we placed oversized planters on each side of the fireplace with large palms inside. Then, we rearranged the furniture, making the access to the room easier. A modern floor lamp and a new slimmer coffee table complete the room. The living and dining space is still really open now, but instead of feeling like two different rooms, it feels like one big room.

Leather cubes and Jennifer's grandmother's chairs (right), reupholstered to really rock, balance the strong colors and drama of the dining room.

Color Story

orange

tangerine

moss green

dark chocolate

Jennifer was not afraid of exciting color. She wanted something with a big impact. The artwork she had already was perfect for her space and was very complementary to the painted walls. The art pops off the wall and makes the green walls look fresher. The green walls make the reds and yellows in the art look intense and rich. Everything is working with the furniture. It's all very modern.

Her grandmother's chairs rock, but they didn't work in their original condition with a beige brocade fabric. What would you do if your grandmother left them to you and you wanted to make them work in your space? Well, we put a kicking fabric on them. We recovered them in a vibrant orange silk, painted the arms and legs in a lacquered black and gave them the lift they needed.

We used a slick tangerine fabric that Jennifer loved for the window treatments in the dining room. We wanted a contemporary line that would distract the eye from the uneven ceiling and also reflect the artwork on the opposite side.

Jennifer's dining room had a very uneven ceiling line with a large window beneath it. We were just terrified to do drapery panels on both sides because everything was just so irregular. We needed to create a window treatment that would distract from the ceiling line. Bright orange Roman blinds on both the living room and dining room windows were the solution. They have the chic Japanese feeling of screens and work in both rooms.

designer**guys** SECRETS

Old Houses and All Their Charms

Old houses are very charming, but often have flaws and imperfections unique to their age. Here are a few tips on dealing with wobbly ceiling lines and cracking plaster.

Uneven Ceiling

To solve this problem at Jennifer's, we placed a piece of masking tape on the wall about one inch from the ceiling. We made sure it was level and then painted the ceiling color right down to that line. That straight line gives you the sense of a false ceiling and camouflages the unevenness of the actual line where the ceiling and walls meet.

Other Options

● Paint the wall and the ceiling the same color.

● Distract the eye from the ceiling by placing a shaped valance on the window. This way, your eye follows along the valance rather than focusing on the wonky ceiling.

● Use patterned fabric for window treatments: it adds some busyness so the eye immediately goes to the fabric and away from the ceiling.

Cracks and Loose Plaster

Old houses are notorious for cracking plaster, which is a normal occurrence caused by houses shifting around. Cracks that run at odd angles from the corners of windows and doors are caused by the house settling over the years. Other wall and ceiling cracks that run in fairly straight lines are often caused by seasonal changes in humidity.

To fix them, you will need three different-size drywall knives ranging from 4 to 10 inches, fiberglass mesh tape, drywall pan, drywall compound, sandpaper and paint. All are available at hardware stores.

1. Gently remove any loose plaster along the cracks with a sharp knife or the edge of a paint scraper.

2. Tape the cracks so they won't reappear within a few months. Use self-adhering fiberglass mesh tape, which is more flexible and longer lasting than paper tape.

3. Apply three or four layers of drywall compound (using a wider knife each time) to cover the tape and disguise the repair. Drywall compound comes in many varieties including dry powders and ready-mix compounds.

4. Finally, when the compound has dried, sand imperfections and uneven spots so your repairs blend into the existing plaster. You are now ready to decorate.

Art Collecting

Collecting art can be a rewarding, though often challenging, endeavor, but it's worth it. Decorating a home with art can instantly warm up a space, add color and inject personality and interest in a room. Here are some tips to add color to your life and home:

Buy art that you love. Do not buy art because you think it's a good investment and somewhere in the future you'll make some money. If you buy something that truly grabs your attention, then it is priceless and will continue to enrich your life forever.

Fine art is a very broad term that does not refer just to oil paintings, but also includes photography and works on paper. Original comic strips, animation cells, vintage music and movie posters, and pop-culture artifacts are also artwork and very collectible. You may have created something yourself, so think about framing and hanging it as well.

Experience art whenever you can. Visit galleries, museums and art shows to help you develop your "eye." Read art and art-history books or books on collecting art. Talk to other art collectors. Subscribe to a few art magazines.

Different galleries offer different price points. A mid-level gallery, for instance, will have artwork priced anywhere from $1,000 to $25,000. Find a dealer that you trust and ask lots of questions and learn about the artists that you are interested in collecting.

As an alternative to commercial galleries and a way to discover emerging artists whose prices aren't yet out of sight, investigate artist-run studios, public galleries, such as government-sponsored art groups and co-ops, and community art fairs and events. Art colleges have yearly showings of graduates' artwork. Find out when the shows are and discover a new talent.

Take works home on approval; it always helps to see the work in your space. Buy what you can afford. Some galleries have payment plans available.

Decorating with Art

You have two choices when it comes to hanging artwork. You can do it yourself and make the decision to put your art wherever you want or you could hire a professional installer. For a nominal fee, anywhere from $75 to $150, a professional installer will come to your home and assist you with proper placement and installation of your artwork. To find a professional installer, consult with an art gallery or look up "Art Consultants" in the yellow pages.

In case you do decide to hang the art yourself, here are some decorating principles to help you add impact and drama to a space.

Hanging Gallery Style. The term "gallery style" refers to artwork hung at eye level, as though you're in a gallery. The nice thing is that you can walk up to each piece and enjoy it individually. This scenario is really effective when used in a long hallway.

Grouping. If you have a large wall, a single print may not give enough impact. Instead, try hanging a series of prints to visually form one large one. The trick to this is to hang them on a strict grid pattern, leaving two inches between each print. This combination works best with even numbers: fours, sixes or eights.

Stacking. Stacking is really effective to visually raise the height of your ceiling. The trick is to hang your first piece quite low and then stack each piece one on top of the other. This dramatic scenario is really effective when hung at the end of a long, narrow hallway.

One of the most common mistakes when hanging art is hanging it too high. How high you hang your paintings depends on whether you will be standing or sitting in the room, but generally 60 inches from the floor is a good place to locate the middle of the painting. For a standing area, you should be looking into the middle of the image, not above or below. If you are hanging art in an area used predominantly for sitting, hang the art lower, because you're viewing it from a lower height.

Other Dos and Don'ts

Wallpaper or wall color should be complementary to the artwork and not competing with it.

Prevent wall damage by planning. If you are considering hanging a group of pieces, use graph paper and sketch the available wall space to see if the art will work well together. Or lay the work on the floor or against the wall where you are thinking of hanging it to get a feel for its placement. This will also let you see how the light will reflect on the work.

Never hang artwork in direct or bright sunlight. It will cause fading and cracking. If you have a room that gets a lot of natural light, special glass with UV protection is now available to protect your artwork.

Do not touch your art with your bare hands. The oils on your skin will damage the work.

Do not store artwork in unheated areas or where the temperature is not controlled, such as attics or basements.

Although oil paintings do not need a protective covering, works on paper and photography should be completely enclosed in a frame, with glass or Plexiglas® as protection. Only acid-free archival materials should be used in the matting and framing.

Jennifer's Conclusion

"I think it's amazing how well my dad's furniture works in here. Now that the space is pulled together, I really enjoy looking at it and I open up the door and say, 'This is mine. It's beautiful. I feel all grown-up.'"

Sleeping Beauty

DITI HAS BROKEN one of the cardinal rules of decorating — never have your office in your bedroom. No wonder she can't sleep. Her bedroom is piled to the ceiling with work files and her bookshelves are crammed with disks and documents. We needed to turn this professional chaos into a personal retreat.

As a busy single mother, Diti's frenetic lifestyle doesn't allow much time for herself. Our challenge is to create a space just for her — a fantasy place that she will never want to leave.

First, we give her some pointers on what is appropriate activity for a bedroom, and then we devise a calming color scheme that will turn her bedroom into a peaceful retreat with a French Country theme. We even talk to an expert about how to get rid of all the clutter. Then we leave the rest to her.

"This is where I try to sleep, but don't because I end up thinking of things I should do for clients and jumping up out of bed and running over to the desk and then realizing it's three o'clock in the morning."

Diti's Wish List

good night's sleep • clutter-free room
• romantic bedroom

Diti's bedroom presented several design challenges. It's a good size, but jam-packed with furniture and all of it dark wood. The only soft item in the room is the fabric on the bed. It would be great to change all the furniture if the budget allowed, but because it doesn't, we need to figure out what to do with all this stuff.

The windows are a problem — one is built out and the other is recessed, and they're at different levels — but because the bedroom faces the street, privacy is a factor. A whole wall of mirrors is overpowering, and then there's all that clutter. It's overwhelming. We get wound up just thinking about it.

A French paint treatment revitalizes and lightens up the dark furniture that overwhelmed the bedroom before (above). Valances and toile de Jouy fabric in blue and white add just the right hint of French Country and cozy up the room (right).

Steven: I'm thinking pretty. Not a little girl's room, but what a little girl's room feels like. Somewhere where she can close the door and be her.

Chris: And that's not to say we're not going to tidy.

Diti loves the color combination of blue and yellow. She also wanted lots of pillows and the bed to be fluffier and cozier, so we decided to explore a French Country look for her bedroom. We shopped for toile, lavender-filled sachets and other accessories from Provence.

We designed a window treatment that overcame the problem of different-size windows. We removed the floor-to-ceiling mirrors from the walls, leaving only one on the closet doors, and followed along as a faux-finish artist made Diti's twenty-year-old maple department-store bedroom suite look like it came out of a 300-year-old French château.

And, of course, we moved the office to another room and hid all the books and papers from view. We hope that now she'll be able to get a good night's sleep.

Valances are a good solution to create balance and equality between the two irregular-size windows. We measured from the floor up to determine where to locate the bottom edge of the valance. We choose a shapely valance for this room to add a more dramatic effect. The drapery fabric is in toile. We left the panels hanging straight down rather than adding tiebacks, which would interrupt the intricate pattern.

To enhance the French Country look, we purchased a bedspread and matching window treatments in a toile de Jouy fabric in blue and white. Decorated with pastoral scenes such as farmyards or picnics, this fabric originated in the eighteenth century. Originally printed on linen, it is often seen now on cotton as well. Toile is French for "cloth." Jouy is short for Jouy-en-Josas, the town in central France where it was first produced.

Diti's walls are painted in a warm vanilla white color to add a sense of calm, and her furniture, now refinished in antique white, brings the whole French Country look together. We can just imagine Diti in a quiet château somewhere in the south of France.

Color Story

■	blue
□	vanilla white
□	antique white

Diti's bedroom shelves were overflowing with stuff. There was so much visual stimulation from all the colors and books, especially at the foot of Diti's bed, that we had to do something. For Diti, it meant that she was constantly bombarded by the hundreds of things she should be reading or doing. We wanted to close the area off or at least tidy it up a bit.

Diti spends a lot of time in her bedroom with her daughter, reading and occasionally watching TV. So even though the clutter-buster lady said, "No TV in the bedroom," we decided to leave it in. Diti can gradually decide herself whether she would like to remove the television, but we didn't want to be the ones to shock her.

Certain books and mementos were special to Diti, so we showcased them on the bookshelves. Other things we placed discreetly away inside wicker baskets. She still has access to all her stuff, but it doesn't look like clutter anymore. And it's a lot tidier.

Wicker baskets organize clutter and calm the room. Cherished possessions now have breathing room on the dresser and shelves. The refinished bureau in an antique white belies its humble origins (right).

designer**guys** SECRETS

Stylishly French

French Country is a very popular decorating style based on the look of rural France. It is informal and comfortable. Think roosters, sunflowers in enamel pitchers, bright colors such as red, yellow and blue, wicker baskets, dented tins, mixed fabrics of stripes and checks, stylized flowers, bistro chairs and crumbling walls.

French Provincial is a more formal style of decorating than French Country. It also refers to a style of furniture developed during the Louis XV period, which includes secretaries and chiffoniers produced from solid woods such as oak and walnut. Rooms are often paneled and are painted or covered with fabric wallpaper or stenciled. Hand-painted linens, embroidery and expensive fabrics are often present.

Parisian style is citified French Provincial and uses luxurious fabrics such as silk and damask. The furniture is very detailed and fine with exquisite carvings, most often painted in a muted color. Fine antiques are often mixed with the best contemporary pieces. Imagine the kind of place a sophisticated Parisian would live in, where the feeling is calm and subdued.

Furniture Make-over

If you can't afford new furniture and want a French antique finish, here's a great technique that makes your pieces look like they naturally changed color with time. You can use this technique on solid wood furniture or veneers.

● Sand furniture lightly, using a medium to light sandpaper to clean off grease and any other debris. If the furniture is particularly sticky or covered in crayons, wash first with an industrial cleaner such as tri-sodium phosphate (TSP), then with clean water.

● Apply one thin coat of a bonder primer sealer in your choice of color. This will allow the paint to adhere to the surface. When it has dried, follow with another coat of latex paint in the same color as the primer. It's better to apply two thin coats rather than one thick coat, which tends to bubble up, get lumpy and show brush strokes. Let dry and sand lightly between coats.

● Very carefully sand the edges to make it look worn like an antique, as though hundreds of hands have touched it through the centuries.

● The last step is to add two glazes. First apply a warm glaze over the whole thing. Then wipe it off with a soft clean cloth while it is still wet. For an antique look, apply a second, darker glaze around the edges and in the grooves. This will make the furniture look believably old. For Diti's furniture, we used an antique glaze and added a raw umber tint to the solution.

● When it is completely dry, seal with a protective coating of a latex varnish.

● Handles. If the original handles are beautiful but the wrong color, apply the same treatment to them as above – a little sanding, some latex paint and the darker glaze only. This technique works on metal or wooden handles.

Clutter Busters

The best way to become an all-round organized person is to simplify your life. Unfortunately, that's a complicated task for those in disarray. We all have lots of stuff in our lives. But that stuff becomes clutter when it starts to affect your lifestyle negatively and cause you stress. Whether it's from procrastination or indecision, holding on to clutter that is taking up more room than you, means it's time to start organizing. Your life can really start to change once you clear the clutter.

Tips

● Contain it. Paper is the biggest culprit, especially in a home office. Try to eliminate it as fast as it comes into your home. If you don't have a recycling system in your neighborhood, get yourself a box and keep it in a closet, underneath the counter or desk or somewhere else out of the way, and use it to throw in junk mail, newspapers, flyers and other unwanted paper. Once a week or biweekly, recycle it.

● Give it a home. Finding places to put stuff is often a problem when storage space is at a minimum. Wicker baskets are a great choice to store mementos and other keepsakes. Magazine holders set on shelves tame loose publications that otherwise clutter up tabletops and floors. The access is still there, but it makes things a lot tidier.

● Toss it. Go through every room, cupboard and drawer in your house at least once a year and get rid of anything that hasn't been used in the last year. Throw it out, donate it to charity or hold a garage sale.

● Closet chaos. Cleaning out your closets is a good place to start. Try on your clothes and ask yourself: Do I like this outfit? Have I worn it in the last year? Does it flatter me? Be brutal.

● Remember the three Rs — refrain, refuse, reject. Harder than getting rid of stuff is saying no to it in the first place. Before you purchase your next item, just imagine where you're going to put it. Think of getting rid of something first before bringing something new home.

Diti's Conclusion

"This room is so beautiful. Morgan loves it too. And that's important to me, because we spend a lot of time in here reading together and occasionally watching TV. It's going to be a paradise."

The Dog Lovers

Puppy Love

NATALIE, WHO'S ONE of our best friends, just bought a new condo and hates the way it looks. So it was up to us to make her fall in love with it. Most of her furniture was given to her by friends and family, so it wasn't anything that she had chosen for herself or for the space.

Natalie wants her place to look pulled together — the way she looks when she's going off to work in one of her business suits — not the current gym look that her condo is sporting at the moment. She wants to feel beautiful in her home and we're going to make that happen for her by starting from the floor and working our way up. And, we're going to do it all within her budget.

We give her the look of Fendi in fabrics, flooring and furniture that even her Great Dane C.C. can't damage. We balance the long, narrow confines of her tiny place and turn the condo down the hall into the belle of the ball.

"C.C. is my 140-pound Great Dane and she just wants to be included in everything. This is very much her home — I'm actually a guest here."

Natalie's Wish List

dog-friendly • fashionable
• an inviting space • happy at home

BEFORE

Natalie didn't want a dining area, but we terrorized her into having one. Where was she going to serve the man who's coming to dinner?

What Natalie did want was a place she could call home for her and C.C. Something beautiful and fashionable and something with a little of her Spanish heritage thrown in — besides the Picasso print she has. Maybe not with castanets and olé, but in an understated, elegant way, like Natalie herself.

What better place to find out what's fashionable than at a fashion show? We hobnob with the trendy crowd and find out what's making its way from the runways to the hallways. Cowboy chic is the forecast for the season, so a pillow with a fringe is one way to capture the moment without spending a fortune. Natalie likes it even more because it reminds her of a mantilla, a Spanish shawl immortalized by Goya in his paintings of high-society women wearing the elegant garment. It has become fashionable once again, particularly as an exquisite and unique bridal veil, which is, we hope, a sign of things to come.

We'd love for Natalie to meet a good man — and we know how hard they are to find.

The guys and Suzanne Boyd, editor of Flare, *take in a fashion show by Misura to see how fashion influences home décor. A lot, as it turns out. There's a definite crossover from fashion to architecture to home décor. If you see it on the runway, you're going to see it in homes and vice versa.*

STEVEN: Natalie's a true fashionista.

CHRIS: A fashion whosta?

STEVEN: A fashionista. She loves high fashion. She spends even more money on shoes than you do.

Floor space is at a premium in Natalie's condo, so a regular-size sofa would be too large. Our solution was to design a narrower-than-normal space-saving one. To do this, we attached a padded backboard directly to the wall and we custom-made a bench and bolster to push up against it — all in the same fabulous you-can't-believe-it's-not-suede Ultrasuede®. On the opposite side of the room we custom-made an oversized frame, which matches the backboard of the sofa. Instead of adding fabric panels, we inserted a smoked mirror. Whoever looks into that mirror is going to feel good. There's just something about smoked glass that does that.

We wanted Natalie's space to feel larger, so we removed the glass partition (see page 154) between the living and dining rooms. But we also wanted the living room and the dining room to be their own separate spaces. So we installed cast stone columns to the entrance of the dining area. Originally, they were a dark terra cotta color. We wanted to lighten them up a bit, so we painted them the same taupe color as the walls. The columns not only separate the rooms, but also give the area the architectural interest it needed with a Mediterranean flair.

To continue to make Natalie's space feel larger and to tie all the rooms together, we chose one type of durable laminate flooring that has the look of wood but will be able to withstand Natalie's high heels and C.C.'s huge claws. We laid it throughout — from the kitchen and the hallway, to the living room and especially to the bathroom because it leads right off the living room. One paint color throughout — taupe — completes the space.

A custom-designed sofa and headboard in a suede-like fabric add elegance and protects against C.C.'s paws. The tray table doubles as a server and elegant stop for drinks.

BEFORE

Well, C.C., the great Great Dane, is beige, and so it's a natural color to choose for Natalie and C.C.'s home. The sofa and its padded wall frame are covered in a soft camel Ultrasuede®, which adds texture to the room. The condo had very little architectural detail, and we wanted the sofa to have an edge to it, something unusual, something that would make beige stand out. The dark frame does this.

Natalie's whole wardrobe (and décor) is slowly turning camel, because C.C. sheds, so we added some chocolate in the standing chrome lamps, chairs and frames to punch things up a bit. It also reminded us of Natalie's hair next to her beige suits, just like when she wears her outfits and C.C. is close to her. We recovered her chairs in a tan vinyl with silver studs that look like pearls. Everything is very warm and inviting about the space — nothing standoffish or aloof about it — just like our great friend, Natalie.

The glass partition between the dining and living room closed the place in. Down it came. Cast stone columns painted the same color as the walls add architectural character as well as separating the two rooms.

Color Story

beige

chocolate

taupe

more beige

glass accents

chrome accents

*A dramatic arrangement of photographs showcases
Natalie having fun with family and friends. Hanging a single
photo wouldn't have had enough impact, so a technique
called grouping, in which a series of prints or photos are hung
to visually form one large one, is used here instead.
Mounting small pictures inside oversized mats and frames
is particularly effective.*

designer**guys** SECRETS

Pet Peeves

If you own a dog or other pet, you probably know all about paw prints on the sofa, scratches on the walls and floors, and fur balls everywhere. But just because you have a pet, it doesn't mean you can't decorate with style. Just research and choose durable finishes for the space.

Fabrics

There are many fabrics and finishes that can stand up to claws and fur. Ultrasuede® is a synthetic fabric that looks and feels just like suede. It's a good bet, because it's washable, stain- and odor-resistant, and looks great. The more you sit on it and the more it gets rubbed, the truer to real suede it starts to look. It will actually soften up just like suede.

Washable cotton or linen slipcovers are another great choice. Make your slipcovers in prewashed fabrics, so they won't shrink when washed. They'll be easier to slip back on the furniture, especially if they are still a bit damp when you do this. White slipcovers might sound like a crazy choice, but you can bleach out the stains.

Floors

Bare floors are the easiest to clean. Light-colored woods won't show the scratches as much as dark wood. Natalie wants hardwood floors for her condo, but will it be practical with C.C.'s

nails, not to mention her high heels? Is there such a thing as a durable hardwood?

There are some hardwoods, such as cherry, mahogany and oak, that might resist marking, but generally, solid wood is not that practical for high-traffic areas, especially if you have a dog. It shows wear and tear much more readily than laminate flooring.

Laminate flooring is a better bet. It is made of actual photographs of real wood that are placed on a fiberboard core, and then covered with a clear scratch-resistant layer of aluminum oxide, the fourth-hardest substance in the world (diamond being number one). The sky's the limit as to what you can use as the actual image on the laminate's surface. It doesn't dent, scratch or fade. You can choose your favorite wood, such as an oak or maple, or go really exotic and choose anything from Australian Cypress to Tasmanian Burlwood.

Carpets

Area rugs should be heavy enough that they don't slide easily and anchored with a nonstick underpad or with furniture.

A berber or a short-pile carpet allows easy removal of pet hair and there are fewer fibers for the pet to pull out.

Natalie's Conclusion

"It's so overwhelming to come into my apartment now. It's a big deal to me. This is my first home."

Mad About You

CARLA IS A very busy media celebrity who has to get up at 4:00 a.m. to host her morning radio show. So, obviously, sleep is at a premium. And, believe us, her bedroom is anything but restful. Right now, she shares it with four males — her husband and three of her four dogs — Buster, Big Red and Bugsy. Whiskey, the fourth dog, sleeps in her own room. Carla wants her bedroom to work hard. It needs to make her and her man happy, accommodate her penchant for shoes, bags and clothing, provide her with a meditation area, lots of cupboard space, a little romantic seating, room to let her dogs sleep comfortably and still have room to sleep.

Carla's daily life is extremely hectic and she wants her bedroom to be a sanctuary with a spiritual feel. We're going for a modern, global look. We get a closet expert in to solve the clothing crunch and ask a feng shui expert to give us some tips. Join us as we turn senseless into sensuous.

"This is the pleasure dome. It's not a beautiful room, but it is large. You can safely land a 747 in here."

160

Carla's Wish List

sanctuary • romantic • calming • great sleeps

STEVEN: Remember, that first day at Carla's? How we laughed all day and got no work done.

CHRIS: She's one funny lady. We could only go back after we had relaxed our stomach muscles.

Carla's bedroom is the size of a small landing strip, but it's in a state of disarray. There are two different floorings, three or four mismatched dressers, an ironing board, chairs, posters and three of her four dogs. So there's not much room for Carla and her husband, Jonathan.

Every other room in the house is decorated but the bedroom. It looks like the bed has just been pushed up against a wall. There's no room on either side of the bed for night tables — no place to even put a lamp. We think the bed is definitely in the wrong place and the dogs have better beds than Carla and Jonathan.

There are two huge pieces of artwork above the bed that aren't being showcased properly. She has a large closet that is a mess, even though she says there is a method to the madness. She wants to keep the fireplace — and rightly so because it's a great area to get cozy — but right now it has been faced in white brick that makes it look like a wedding cake, plus it's in the corner, which is another challenge. We need to empty the room entirely and call in the feng shui expert to help us plan the space so that positive chi can flow.

Carla and Jonathan share their bedroom with three dogs (see their little doggie beds at the foot of the bed?) Pets are very good feng shui. They stimulate the chi and keep the energy flowing in the home. And we could all use some of that in the bedroom, right?

BEFORE

BEFORE

The feng shui expert has been and it's official. The bed is definitely located in the wrong place for Carla and Jonathan. Even the direction it faces is incorrect. The fireplace in the southwest corner is excellent, because it's facing one of Carla's good directions (see *Feng Shui*, page 171). And what better way to meditate than in front of a fire?

The feng shui expert has even recommended the colors we should use — earthy tones with a little bit of red and a lot of gold to enforce the positive energy within the room. She also advised us to stay away from chrome or glass. So we come up with an alternative plan for night tables — floating shelves covered in woven leather, mounted directly to the wall to act as bedside tables. We've also custom designed a headboard in the same material. With all these rich textures, Carla's bed is sure to be the focal point of the room and the perfect place for her to relax and unwind.

We're stuck on what route to go with respect to the floors, though — all hardwood or all carpeting? We want it soft underfoot, but wall-to-wall carpet can be difficult to keep clean, especially with four dogs.

Carla's bedroom is all about textures — on the bed cover, floor cushions, carpeting and headboard. With the room tidied up and simplified, the bed is now sure to be the focal point of the room, unlike before (above), where so much disparate furniture had created chaos and no focal point.

Normally, in a room with a fireplace, the fireplace would be the natural focal point. But in Carla's bedroom, we had a few challenges. Number one, the fireplace was on an angle. And number two, we had to reposition the bed. Our solution was to downplay the fireplace by drywalling over the brick. We then custom made a large, dramatic headboard, making the bed the new focal point.

The nude sculptures over Carla's bed were a wedding present from a friend. They are really important to her, so we wanted to give them a sense of importance in the room. We created oversized shadow boxes to go around them. To keep them light in weight, we used Plexiglas® instead of glass. And now that they're up, they really have a museum-like quality.

When choosing what to put above the fireplace, we didn't want anything too dramatic that would take attention away from the bed. We decided on an airy metal sculptural sphere.

We finally chose to replace the floors in light brown maple hardwood and laid on top two beautiful rugs, a massively long runner and a huge square one under the bed.

Carla's a very spiritual and tactile person. With that in mind, we had to find the perfect primitive pieces to complete her global, modern look. We selected items from Tibet, Burma and India, including chakra chimes and a Tibetan prayer bowl.

The feng shui expert advised against chrome or glass for Carla, but everybody needs a night table. Floating shelves covered with a very durable woven leather fabric are the perfect alternative — they match the custom-designed headboard (left). Silk and sateen pillows (right) tossed on the floor in front of the fireplace make this the perfect place of meditation.

Bedrooms are people's sanctuaries. It's a place where one can be totally enveloped in luxury. Warmth and textures bring romance into a person's life. That's why we've used rich colors of gold and burgundy and luscious textures in silks and satins.

Refinishing the fireplace created a lot of physical mess, but after that had been cleaned, and the hardwood and cupboards both installed, the room took on a whole new look. It now has great bones. The crème brûlée color of the cabinets ties in beautifully with the maple floors. A window covering hung from floor to ceiling gives the room an ethereal touch, sensuous and floating in burnt sienna linen that has a shimmering quality. The bed, repositioned according to the feng shui expert's advice, is backed by a luxurious mini-basket-weave leather headboard, also in burnt sienna, that matches the floating night table. Two 1930s-style slipper chairs in the same cream color as the walls replace the previous chairs and anchor the fireplace. Now Carla has her own little corner of the world — a place that's her special utopia where she can even do yoga in her heels.

A trendy rough-textured abstract woodblock table contrasts well with the sleek, pared-down contemporary chairs; together they create a cozy area in front of the window.

Color Story

cream

crème brûlée

burnt sienna

burgundy

beige

Closets

You can never have enough closet space. And in Carla's case, enough pants and dresses. And shoes and gloves and purses and hairpins and things and stuff and…We had to get the advice of a closet expert, who tells us the closet was definitely not designed for Carla's needs. She has a lot of clothes. And even though she does have a system, it's one that requires her to be ironing her clothes all the time as she pulls them out. Thus the obvious high-profile placement of the ironing board smack dab in the middle of the bedroom.

Our expert not only looked at what was being stored in the closet, but also at the empty spaces. What she saw was a bunch of clothes that were really crammed in and then a lot of empty spaces up above. The solution was to build right up to the ceiling, adding additional shelving so that all the space was usable.

Clothes that aren't needed on a daily basis, that are out of season or that just need to be stored can go on the top out-of-reach shelves. We spread it all out and allocated a place for everything. Smartly, it's all fully adjustable. So if Carla wants to move a rod up above one of the shelves and provide an extra shelf down at the bottom for perhaps her gym bag, she can.

designer**guys** SECRETS

Feng Shui

Many people believe there is a connection between your environment and your well-being. Some places radiate a sense of warmth and comfort, while others create a feeling of uneasiness. The 3,000-year-old Chinese art of feng shui explains this phenomenon. Feng shui, which means wind and water, can teach us a lot about decorating our homes, because it is essentially about the art of design and placement. It addresses the principles of balancing our life's energy, or chi, in our living space by harnessing the positive energy within our interior and exterior environments.

The first thing our feng shui consultant, Susan Chow, did was to ask for Carla and Jonathan's birth dates. This is very important because a birth date gives a feng shui expert your Life Kua or Birth Number, which then explains your energy and where the most auspicious locations for furniture or rooms would be. This is how our expert discovered that Carla's bed was located in the wrong place.

In Carla's case, Susan had two Kua numbers to consider because Carla is married. Although the numbers can often represent the same direction, there are times when they are different. This situation is dealt with on a case-by-case basis, depending on who in the relationship would benefit the most from the placement. If someone has started a new business or career, for instance, the bed would be positioned in his (or her) favor and perhaps something else in the room placed for balancing the other person's chi.

Susan was kind enough to provide us with instructions and a chart so that you too can calculate your Life Kua Number. Start by adding the last two digits of the year you were born to get a single-digit number. For instance, if you were born in 1965, add 6 and 5 to get 11, then add 1 plus 1 to equal 2.

Women add 5 to your single-digit number. In this case, 2 plus 5 equals 7. This is your Life Kua Number.

Men subtract your number from 10. So in the case of 1965, it would be 10 minus 2 for a Life Kua Number of 8.

If your number comes to 5, males take the number 2 and females the number 8. Don't ask us why. Some things in life remain mysterious.

The numbers are divided into West and East Groups. Use this chart below to figure out your best directions.

	West Group	East Group
Life Kua Number	2, 6, 7, 8	1, 3, 4, 9
Good Directions	W, NW, SW, NE	N, S, SE, E
Bad Directions	N, S, SE, E	W, NW, SW, NE

Once you have your best directions, place your bed against a wall that faces that direction. In your office or when you're in a meeting, sit facing your good direction. The only change to this rule is in the kitchen. The stove should be located against a bad direction but facing a good one.

Here are a few simple ideas that feng shui practitioners believe can enhance the energy in your bedroom.

Make sure the head of your bed is against the wall. If your bedroom is designed so that you have to place the bed on a diagonal, make sure you have a headboard to rest against.

Headboards should be unadorned – flat or padded are best. If you have a wrought-iron or carved headboard, make sure you have pillows placed up against it.

Do not place your bed under a window or ceiling fan. Both of these things will disturb your sleep by upsetting the balance of energy around you during the night. If you must sleep under a window, place thick coverings on the windows.

Although water is considered good luck (see below), it is not a good idea to have water in your bedroom – no fish tanks or fountains. A vase with water and flowers is okay, though. If your bed is beside a bathroom, make sure you keep the bathroom door closed and the toilet seat down.

Keep your bedroom uncluttered (see *Clutter Busters*, page 144).

Other Good Feng Shui Symbols
Water
Flowing water, such as in fountains and aquariums, is very soothing. Feng shui experts believe water is used to harness energy to bring good fortune. Aquariums or fountains are often placed in Asian restaurants to enhance their prosperity. Water is a very powerful symbol. If objects containing water are not positioned correctly, they could cause more harm than good. It is best to consult with a feng shui expert before placing any water in or around your environment.
Pets
Pets are very good feng shui. A dog or a cat that is allowed to roam around freely in your home adds a continued presence to your environment, even when you're not there, stimulating the chi and keeping the energy in the home flowing.

Things to Avoid
Poison Arrows
In Carla's bedroom, the best wall for the bed had another adjacent wall jutting out from it, which, once the bed was repositioned, would point at the bed. The wall had to come down otherwise it would act as a poison arrow toward the bed, which according to feng shui would enforce negative energy. It is basically anything that has a sharp angle pointing directly toward you such as a wall or the corner of furniture.
Mirrors
Mirrors can be good, especially to enhance a small space, but in a bedroom, do not allow them to reflect the bed. A mirror reflection causes your chi to become unstable and could cause uneasiness and squabbles with a partner, as well as health issues.
Overhead Beams
Do not sleep under exposed overhead beams or ceiling ducts. They will cause sleepless nights and disagreements between couples. If you have beams or ducts in your bedroom, place drapes over them or cover them with a false ceiling.

Carla's Conclusion

"I really believe everybody has to have a little corner of the world, a little home that's a utopia. And now I have mine."

The Renovators

Loft and Found

WE'VE KNOWN ROD for fifteen years. He's a great guy and a great friend. Rod loves his open-concept loft and so do we. The huge windows, high ceilings and three concrete architectural pillars are all magnificent. We wouldn't have changed a thing, but Rod has asked us to renovate and redecorate. He wants his place to have a nightclub or cocktail-bar feel — an environment where his friends can gather and share a drink and good times.

How do you take someone's home and turn it into a club? Nightclubs are about cool little hangout areas for smaller groups of people rather than lots of people gathered around in the living room. We can take away a certain sense of home — no living room, dining room or den. Rod says he doesn't need a kitchen because he doesn't cook, but he still has to live here. How much function do you still have to have?

Before we start swinging sledgehammers, there's much to consider. First we must investigate the repercussions of removing walls and cupboards. What to do about the hall closet? Right now, it blocks the view of the three stunning columns, but it holds so much stuff. Can we rip it out? What are the floors like underneath, what about the wall it's attached to? But most of all — what about storage? We have to check the electrical wiring in the walls and the condition of the floors beneath the kitchen island. Can we remove the kitchen island? All will be answered as we take your average loft out for a night on the town.

"I love the concrete floors. That was one of the things that really attracted me to the place, along with the pillars and stuff. And I loved the color when I first moved in, but you know what, I don't look good next to this color."

Rod's Wish List

nightclub atmosphere • fireplace • minimal kitchen

CHRIS: This is a huge space, but it's not large enough to hold fifteen contractors, all working here at once.

STEVEN: Yeah, you're going bananas.

CHRIS: I'm about to snap like a dry twig on a dead tree.

Rod says he doesn't need a formal kitchen or the traditional cabinets because he doesn't cook and the kitchen island sweeps right into the living room.

Rod passionately dislikes the red brick color on the walls. It's too dark and too intense. Plus the color doesn't continue all the way up the fourteen-foot walls, but stops at about ten feet. You have high ceilings, why not accentuate the height?

Although he doesn't have one now, Rod was told his loft is fitted for a gas fireplace. He would really like one, because he grew up with one and likes the hominess a fireplace will bring. The fireplace is a challenge, though, because the whole notion of a fireplace is coziness. We have to create an ambience that isn't about roasting marshmallows because that wouldn't be very nightclub-like, now, would it?

BEFORE

The open-concept bedroom that is raised above the rest of the loft worked for Rod when he first moved in (left), but now he feels like he's sleeping in a fishbowl. He needs some privacy. Because there isn't a window or skylight in the bedroom, Rod didn't want to block off the light completely in this area. We created a thick, clear-tempered glass wall as a divider (right), covered with blinds that can be rolled down for the evening and left up during the day.

The majestic wall of windows in Rod's loft were just one
of many focal points. A massive nine-foot mirror on the
wall opposite the huge fireplace not only balances the
room, but reflects the windows as well. Classic Barcelona
chairs and a bench — all in black leather and designed
by Mies van der Rohe — anchor the seating area.

Living in a disco sounded like a good idea at the time, but mixing all these residential needs with a nightclub look was driving us crazy. The key was to give Rod all the things he wanted, but we also had to convince him that he still needed a kitchen, even though he said he didn't want one. He still has to live there and the place still has to be functional.

The problem with the open-concept nightclub idea was how to incorporate a kitchen without it looking too much like a kitchen. Plus, his kitchen is right in the middle of his living room. It's an open-concept loft, so the kitchen had to remain practical and functional yet not take away from the main stage that is the living room. To achieve this, we removed the kitchen island and chose a high-gloss finish for the kitchen cabinets in thunder gray, which matches the wall color exactly. The cabinets are hung in a straight grid pattern right to the ceiling, which accentuates the height and makes room for additional storage. (The top cupboards are obviously really high, so this is a good area to keep stuff that's not used every day.) Rather than handles to open the cupboards, we gave them a touch latch — you just have to touch them and they pop open. This non-use of hardware makes them feel like a paneled wall instead of kitchen cabinets.

So we managed to give Rod a kitchen that didn't look like a kitchen, but practicality won when it came to the hall closet. It stayed. Ripping it out would have meant losing an incredible storage facility, plus the floors and walls would have been so damaged that the extra work involved was just out of the question. We utilized some space beside it, though, to place a little banquette and table — another club-like area for people to gather.

Rod didn't want a kitchen, so down came the island that intruded on the precious living room space (right). The unique kitchen with cabinets designed on a strict grid pattern mimic the grid-like effect of the windows. Black appliances practically disappear in the kitchen that Rod didn't want. He can move the small, round table out of the way for large gatherings.

183

What's the focal point in Rod's loft? This was a question we grappled with for quite a while, but really, the answer is just about everything. In a space like Rod's, there really isn't a focal point. When you first walk in, the windows are overwhelming. Then there's the enormous height and drama of the fireplace and huge architectural pillars. There's such a sense of theater throughout the space that everything has to have an impact.

One of Rod's requests was a fireplace in his loft. When designing the look of it, we took inspiration from the gray pitted concrete columns that were already here. Its large scale perfectly mimics the pillars on the opposite wall. The fireplace had to be huge to hold its presence in the room against the grand scale of the columns, tall windows and high ceilings. To visually balance the weight of the fireplace, we placed a nine-foot mirror on the opposite wall.

Rod wanted a fireplace, but a slick, modern fireplace with no tactile presence would have been too cold and sterile. This fireplace takes its raw, pitted texture cue from the loft's three large columns. The craftsman who built it first made a wooden frame to the designed shape of the fireplace and then faced it with hand-cast stone. Now it's a natural gray stone color, heavy and very tall and able to hold its own against the columns. The painting adds a splash of color.

When we were thinking of the color scheme for Rod's loft, we kept in mind his request that the space should look like a nightclub. Usually nightclubs are decorated in a way that makes them more of a backdrop or a stage for the people who are there. We really wanted to tone down Rod's environment and make it very neutral, so that when he did entertain, the people would be the stars and everything else would pull back.

We painted the huge fourteen-foot walls from floor to ceiling in a dark gray. A matching thunder gray — in high gloss — appears on the kitchen cabinets. Black appliances dramatize the kitchen and black high-gloss floors stretch throughout the loft. The pitted concrete fireplace matches the three huge columns. A red abstract painting adds color to one wall and two red Persian-like carpets run along the hallway leading into the living room.

We wanted the furniture in Rod's loft to be sleek and streamlined, so we shopped for some classics. A black leather backless daybed really attracted us and seemed more appropriate for Rod's space than a traditional sofa. You can sit back to back, sit on either side, plus it has a club feel. We recovered two of his favorite chairs in black Ultrasuede®. So bring on the red wine! Nothing can stain or hurt this stuff. Because Rod is such a big fan of Mies van der Rohe, we invested in two black leather chairs with chrome legs designed by the famous architect and furniture designer to round out the seating.

The kitchen with its slick, high-gloss cabinets happens just to the right of the fireplace. The New Millennium meets the Renaissance for the Millennisance look. Even though Rod describes himself as "not-a-sit-down-dinner kind of guy," he now has two places to dine if he changes his mind: the small round table in the kitchen area or the cozy banquette in the hall.

Color Story

dark gray

black

concrete

red accents

*An inviting banquette fills the otherwise wasted space in the hall adjacent
to the closet (above) looking and feeling very much like a quiet intimate
zone in a nightclub — perfect for a special tête-à-tête. The bedroom
(right) is hidden behind thick, clear-tempered glass, which during
the day lets light in from the huge living room windows.*

Rod's Conclusion

"I was stunned when I walked in. It had exactly the feel I wanted. I love the way the kitchen is just hidden and the fireplace is so striking. I knew the guys would work their magic and they did. It's amazing."

designer**guys** SECRETS

How to Survive a Reno

We renovated Rod's whole loft in one fell swoop. Tore out the kitchen, replaced the floors, built him a new fireplace. And all while Rod was out of town. It's very unusual for the client not to be around. Rod trusted us and so he disappeared, but in most cases, it's best to be in constant touch with your contractor, designer or architect and to make yourself available whenever needed. If renovation plans are in your near future, here are a few things to consider before you knock down a wall or replace a sink.

If you are on a tight budget, you may decide to do your renovations in stages. Or, money may be

no object and you're planning to do the whole thing at once. Either way, it's essential to establish an overall plan of action at the outset that takes your entire house into account before any work commences. Without a master plan, there's a danger that, over time, the project will gradually expand into something far bigger than you can afford. Would-be renovators should make a list of all the things they want to do and all the alterations they want to make – just like Rod did when he told us he wanted a fireplace and didn't need a kitchen. Then, you're best to get a designer or architect to draw up plans for the contractor (whose credentials and references you've checked out) to use in achieving your goals.

A good plan also illustrates the necessity of doing certain things that might otherwise be overlooked. In all renovations, there are some initial steps in the construction process that are essential, but they are not going to give visible results, because they are connected with unseen elements such as heating, electrical and plumbing functions. For example, if an addition is part of the renovation plans, a new furnace may be needed to look after the extra heat requirements. Kitchen renovations require you to take a hard look at the wiring capabilities of the house. A new, larger electrical panel may be called for.

Having to spend money on this first "invisible" phase may disappoint you, but don't be tempted to skip this part. It's critical to have the proper services in place. Once these hidden steps are accomplished, you can move on to the more exciting visible work.

There is no doubt that there is some degree of physical, mental and emotional stress involved with a renovation. Family life can be

disrupted and there is a certain loss of privacy. For some, it feels as if they're living out of a suitcase forever. But in the end, it very much depends on individual temperaments. Here are some useful tips, so you won't be fazed by your renovation, especially if you're living there while it's going on. We can't all be like Rod and fly the coop.

● Pack up your treasured belongings in sturdy boxes, label them and store far away from the area being renovated.

● Keep your good clothes in zippered bags, and protect your furniture and furnishings from plaster dust and debris by covering them with heavy-gauge plastic sheeting.

● Plan your renovation carefully so you don't end up taking a sponge bath in the kitchen sink. Leave the old tub and shower in place until the new tub is installed, so you have a place for washing up. If the kitchen is your current target area, plan how to survive without it. Move the refrigerator to another room, use a microwave oven, hot plate or barbecue for cooking and wash the dishes in your bathroom sink or laundry tub. Make similar alternative plans for other rooms under renovation.

● Be sure to tell your contractor what you prize in your garden so that he will respect it.

● Tell your neighbors of your plans before any work begins. They need reassurance that any proposed additions will not block their sun patterns or suddenly give you a bird's-eye view into their private spaces. Their cooperation and patience will be necessary if work crews set up ladders on their property and equipment gets noisy.

● Clean up at the end of every day.

● Keep good lines of communication open with your contractor and tradespeople. Establish who is in control, who is the chief liaison person, who makes major decisions (you? your partner? the contractor? the architect/designer?)

● Be flexible and deal calmly with unforeseen emergencies that are certain to occur.

● Don't make changes along the way or agree to extras: the domino effect kicks in and you don't know what other things will be affected by these new decisions. You can be certain that changes will add to the cost.

● Keep a list of things that seem wrong or need adjustment and go over it with your contractor all at once. Don't pick away about things a little at a time.

● Have a place to relax and watch TV somewhere away from the area being renovated.

● Keep your sense of humor.

● Keep an eye on your pets; renovations disrupt their routines, too.

● Take weekend holidays – not extended ones, while the renovations are in progress.

● Don't regret long weekends when your work crews are gone for three days; you and your neighbors need a break from the noise, mess and disruption, and the crews need to refresh themselves. They will work better after a break.

● Save some money for furnishings after the renovations are finished, because new surroundings look bleak if left unfurnished.

The Kitchen Reno

If your kitchen appliances and cabinets have long passed their "best before" dates or the room no longer works for your personal style or it fails to function efficiently, you're probably in the market for a culinary overhaul. Big or small, major or minor, a kitchen renovation can be lots of fun – or straight from hell – and you can play a big part in which it'll be.

For a smooth reno experience, make a wish list of all the features you want in a new kitchen and the reasons you want them. Put them in order of priority in case you have to knock off some at the bottom of the list for money or space reasons. Have a good idea of the amount of money you want to spend on the project.

Draw a floor plan of your existing kitchen. Mark it up with the location of your appliances, sinks, electrical outlets, windows and doors. Measure the perimeter of the room to help you locate these items exactly on your plan. Note how high the window ledges are off the floor. Write all this on your plan.

Discuss your list with and show your plan to a designer, architect or kitchen planner (most large building centers have experts on staff and computer software to design a new kitchen; kitchen planners are also listed in the yellow pages of the telephone book). Work out together how to achieve your goals.

Give some thought to the following questions: How many people will be cooking at one time? Does the kitchen need to withstand hard use by many people or will it get limited use? Do you want an eat-in kitchen? Do you like the current layout? If you can swing it, would you like an island or L-shaped counter extension? Are there other activities besides meal prep and eating that might take place in the kitchen, such as school homework, sewing projects, plant potting, laundry? Do you hope to enlarge the space? Do you need new appliances? Do you need to create more storage space? More counter space? At present, do you have adequate venting, lighting, electrical outlets, sinks? What "look" do you love – traditional, contemporary, country or retro?

Hire a reputable contractor with whom you are comfortable working. Be sure he or she comes with good references; check out previously completed jobs if possible. Agree on a price, but be aware that costs will likely be at least 10 percent more than you think. Draw up a work schedule together, so you know the time frame you both are committing yourselves to.

Seven Things to Know

1. Bigger is not always better. Some of the "best" kitchens are small. What counts is the smart ergonomic layout of kitchen elements (sinks, stove, refrigerator, counters, cabinets) so that the cook – or cooks – who work there can do so effectively and efficiently without scurrying all over the room or bumping into each other.

2. Base cabinets are usually 36 inches high and 24 inches deep. Wall-mounted upper cabinets are usually 12 to 15 inches deep and set 16 to 18 inches above the countertop. It's a good idea to have some counter space at least 15 inches wide adjacent to the refrigerator to use when transferring food in or out of the fridge. A cabinet or shelves above the fridge are handy to store infrequently used items. The dishwasher should be less than 25 inches away from the sink.

3. The amount of storage space you need depends on the amount of equipment you have – plus an allowance for additional kitchen stuff you'll acquire in the future. The amount of counter space you need depends on your personal style in the kitchen: Do you bake a lot? Entertain a lot? Are you neat and tidy or messy?

4. Open shelving will save you money but is high-maintenance: you'll need to keep the contents looking tidy and they will likely get covered with dust and grime.

5. Locating sinks or stoves on an angle in a corner is a smart space-saving technique. Appliance garages also make good use of corner space. Be sure there's an electrical outlet nearby.

6. A toe-kick – the recessed space at the bottom of lower cabinets – allows your feet to be positioned slightly under the cabinets and puts your body close to the countertop work surface. If you do not have a toe-kick, project the countertop three inches over the edge of the lower cabinets to compensate.

7. If you're counting on having an island, you need 30 inches clearance to be able to open your dishwasher door and 42 inches clearance to open the oven door.

Easy Upgrades

No money for a kitchen reno? Try some or all of these quick tricks to freshen up the room and make you feel better about the space:

- Paint the existing cabinets

- Buy new cabinet doors and drawer fronts

- Add decorative molding strips to existing drawers and doors

- Change the knob and pull hardware

- Change the window treatments: consider a Roman shade or shutters

- Repaint the walls or hang wallpaper

- Replace the countertop

- Lay a new floor

- Install new lighting

- Install a new sink and faucets

Renovating Your Bathroom

Bathrooms used to play second fiddle to the rest of the house, but not anymore. A bathroom renovation is now one of the most popular home-improvement projects. Whether you go all the way and renovate or just add a few quick touch-ups, it's worth improving a room that gives you so much pleasure.

Before you start renovating, think about what your bathroom needs and budget are. You may be surprised at how much of your budget must go toward "hidden" work that you'll never see, but must be done, before you get to the fun, decorating part. Be sure that you understand what needs to be done and whether or not it is too complicated or time consuming for a do-it-yourselfer. Here are a few things to consider before you knock down a wall or replace a tub.

Renovation

Are you thinking of enlarging your bathroom? Structural changes can be very costly if done improperly. Do not knock down any walls before talking to an expert. Things to look out for:

Walls

Load-bearing walls cannot be knocked down. If you proceed with improper structural changes, your new additions or loads could stress the structure and cause the wall to settle or collapse.

If the walls contain plumbing or electrical, you need to make sure they can be rerouted before bringing the wall down.

Make sure existing walls and any new walls are deep and strong enough for installation of grab bars, new windows, plumbing or ducts. You can build out walls to accommodate these features. Insufficient wall cavities prevent proper insulation and could result in cold surfaces that cause discomfort and are prone to condensation, which can lead to mold growth.

Be sure, too, to insulate exterior walls properly. You don't want frozen pipes when temperatures dip.

Plumbing and Electrical

If your house is more than thirty years old, your plumbing and electrical may be outdated and need upgrading. Houses built before 1950 often have lead piping that may pose a health hazard.

Call in a plumber to investigate any leaky taps, water stains or mold growth. A plumber will be able to determine whether the moisture is coming from a plumbing leak or high humidity. Repair or replace all water-damaged or deteriorating elements. Unresolved water problems may cause renovations to deteriorate quickly and cause mold growth to continue.

Cracks

Look for cracks or slopes in the floor or supporting members. Do not ignore these problems. If you just tile or drywall over them, you may have recurring problems.

Floors

Be sure the weight-bearing capabilities of the floors and joists are strong enough to support a huge or heavy tub with a big-water capacity if you are planning on installing one. You don't want the tub to end up in the living room.

Quick Fix-ups

If a big renovation is not in your near future, but your bathroom needs a little help now, consider these quick alternatives:

● Replace outdated, leaky or cracked fixtures.

● Decorate your bathroom window with shutters or Roman blinds for ease of raising and lowering. Add a matching shower curtain.

● Apply a fresh coat of paint in full or semigloss to make cleanup easier.

● Replace the hardware on cupboards, towel racks and toilet holders.

● Install a new mirror with a fabulous frame.

● Reglaze an old tub whose porcelain is worn or damaged.

● Use wicker baskets for storing towels and toilet paper.

● Paint the floor or replace the bath mat with something fresh and new.

Index

Acknowledgments

THERE ARE SO many talented people to thank for helping us create the beautiful spaces contained in this book. They include homeowners, designers, artisans, tradespeople and craftspeople.

First we would like to thank editor Carol Sherman and designer Andrew Smith of Smith Sherman Books. Without their tireless dedication to this project, there would be no book. Also thanks to Mary Darling, Clark Donnelly, all our friends at WestWind Pictures and Allan Magee. Without them, there would be no designer**guys** television show.

Thank you to the homeowners who so generously allowed us into their homes and are featured in this book: Sue and Tim Bowen, Rodney Bruce, Carla Collins, Diti Dumas, Jamie Erickson, Liza Finlay, Jennifer Harkness, Kirsti Jansson, Bernie Macmillan, Jill Merry, Natalie Sanchez and Rianne Simo.

Thanks to the following experts who gave us so much valuable information for this book: Darren Alexander, Tatar Alexander Gallery; Susan Chow, Feng Shui National Inc.; Jim Connelly, Masterpieces Inc.; Hank Dejong, Sheridan Nurseries Ltd.; Estelle Gee, Orderly Lives; Chris Laidlaw, Peacock Flooring; and Lisa Nicholl, BB Bargoons.

An added thank you to the following people, who contributed to this book in so many ways: Andrew Bottecchia, Jackie Brown, Michelle Bryson, Kim Dal Bianco, Brehana Darling, David Dembroski, Brett Donnelly, Bernice Eisenstein, Ryan Francoz, Doug Gibson, Ene Haabniit, Pat Kennedy, Joan Mackie, Marc Simard, Monica Sisson, Erik Tanner and Daniella Zanchetta.

*"designer**guys**"* art director Andrew Bottecchia consults with Chris and Steven

WestWind Pictures Ltd.
2 Pardee Avenue, Suite 203
Toronto, ON M6K 3H5 Canada
(416) 516-4414
www.westwindpictures.com

designerguys
www.designerguys.com

Smith Sherman Books Inc.
533 College Street, Suite 402
Toronto, ON M6G 1A8 Canada
(416) 960-3646
studio@pagewavegraphics.com

*For international publishing rights
for this book, please contact Andrew Smith
at Smith Sherman Books Inc.*

McClelland & Stewart Ltd.
481 University Avenue, Suite 900
Toronto, ON M5G 2E9 Canada
(416) 598-1114

*For bulk or special sales of this book, please contact
Marlene Fraser at Random House Canada*

Many thanks to the following stores and sponsors for their invaluable contributions:

Adanac Glass
  www.adanacglass.com
Angus & Company
Artemide Canada Ltd.
  www.artemide.com
BB Bargoons
  www.bbbargoons.com
Black & Decker
  www.blackanddecker.com
Bullet
  www.bullethome.com
Caban/Club Monaco
  www.clubmonaco.com
Canac Kitchens
  www.canackitchens.com
Closet Factory
  www.closetfactory.com
D & E Lake Ltd.
  www.delake.com
Dig This
Drapes & Sew Much More
Drew Harris *(painting page 58)*
DuVerre
  www.duverre.com
eatons
  www.eatons.com
ELTE
  www.elte.com
En Provence
  www.shopenprovence.com
Farrow & Ball
  www.farrow-ball.com
Feng Shui National Inc.
  www.susanchow.com
Flare
  www.flare.com

Harry Rosen
  www.harryrosen.com
Harvest spa
  www.harvestspa.com
Holt Renfrew
  www.holtrenfrew.com
Horsefeathers Antiques
  hfeather@ftconline.ca
Hugo Boss
  www.hugoboss.com
IKEA Toronto
  www.ikea.ca
James Lahey *(painting, page 44)*
Jane Hall
  The Voice of Color
  (dining room chairs, pages 32 and 33)
  www.janehallthevoiceofcolor.com
Jonathan Dueck *(painting, page 129)*
LA Design
  www.livingartsdesign.com
L'Atelier
Lenz Entertainment
Loomis & Toles
  www.loomisandtoles.com
Machine Age
  www.machineagemodern.com
Masterpieces Inc.
  www.masterpiecesstudio.com
Maytag
  www.maytag.com
Misura Inc.
  www.misurainc.com
Morba
  www.morba.com
Nestings Home Furnishings
Nestings Kids Junior Homestore
  www.nestingskids.com
Nienkämper
  www.nienkamper.com

Orderly Lives
  www.orderlylives.net
Pack-Rat
Palazzetti
  www.palazzetti.com
Peacock Flooring
  www.peacockflooring.com
Putti
  putti@sympatico.ca
Restoration Hardware
  www.restorationhardware.com
Roots Canada Ltd.
  www.roots.com
Sheridan Nurseries
  www.sheridannurseries.com
Siena Design
  www.masterpiecesstudio.com
Silva Upholstering
Smoothcrete
  www.smoothcrete.com
Style at Home
  www.styleathome.com
Tatar Alexander Gallery
  www.tataralexander.com
Teatro Verde
  www.teatroverde.com
The Door Store
  www.thedoorstore.ca
UpCountry
  www.upcountry.ca
Urban Mode
  www.urbanmode.com
Wilsonart Canada
  www.wilsonart.com
Woven Art Studios
  www.wovenart.com
WTF Group Ltd.
  www.wtfgroup.com